THE FIRST PART OF THE HISTORY
OF KING HENRY THE FOURTH

The First Part of the History of King Henry the Fourth

WILLIAM SHAKESPEARE

EDITED BY H. M. RICHMOND

THE UNIVERSITY OF CALIFORNIA

BERKELEY

THE BOBBS-MERRILL COMPANY, INC.

INDIANAPOLIS · NEW YORK

CONTENTS

CONTENTS

Introduction

THE HISTORICAL BACKGROUND

Shakespeare dramatized the history of late medieval England in two sequences, each comprising four plays. Both his tetralogies, as the sequences are called, derive ultimately from the actual events that surrounded and resulted from the deposition in 1399 of King Richard II (1367–1400; crowned, 1377). The bitter conflicts over the succession that followed this event, mingled with interludes of warfare in France, culminated in the Wars of the Roses (1455–1485), which raged between two rival branches of the Plantagenet dynasty—the Lancastrians, whose badge was a red rose, and the Yorkists, whose emblem was a white rose. The numerous battles and assassinations of this period ended in the extinction of the male line of both branches of the Plantagenet family. The last Yorkist King, Richard III, was defeated at Bosworth in 1485 by the last Lancastrian claimant, a descendant in a female line who bore the Welsh family name of Tudor. He became Henry VII, marrying the Yorkist princess Elizabeth; and their son became Henry VIII, father of Shakespeare's own Queen Elizabeth.

Although one is tempted to read the eight plays about these events as an unbroken sequence, Shakespeare began with the last phase of the period, when England was ruled first by Henry VI and then by his Yorkist enemies Edward IV and Richard III. This phase ended with the establishment of the Tudor dynasty. In his later and more mature tetralogy, Shakespeare went backward in time to seek the roots of all the disorders, beginning with *Richard II*. In this play he shows the difficulties facing the kingdom of an immature if intelligent ruler (patron, historically, of Chaucer); Richard succeeded prematurely to the throne of his grandfather, Edward III, because of the early death of his father, the Black

Prince. The main facts of the case have always been known: Richard's authority was enviously challenged at various times by older relatives, who felt he was inadequate as King; and threats of deposition provoked by his irresponsibility led ultimately to civil war and to a loss of order throughout the kingdom. In 1397 Richard unwisely protected himself from challenges and talk of deposition by having the most hostile of his uncles, the Duke of Gloucester, assassinated. Richard's cousin, Henry Bolingbroke, then apparently challenged as a traitor the man supposed to be immediately responsible for the murder, the Duke of Norfolk, who charged Bolingbroke with treason. Both men were exiled, presumably as a way of hushing things up and avoiding further challenges; but Richard was later foolhardy enough, upon the death of his uncle John of Gaunt (Duke of Lancaster, and regent during Richard's minority), to seize the Lancastrian inheritance that should have passed to Bolingbroke, John's son. This injustice gave Bolingbroke a pretext for returning from exile while Richard was away in Ireland and for exploiting popular dissatisfaction with the high-handed actions of the King. The insurrection was successful; Richard was forced to abdicate in 1399, and in effect Parliament elected Henry in his place. Richard died the next year at Pontefract, where, according to rumor, he was murdered with Henry IV's connivance. These are the main historical facts covered by Shakespeare's play *Richard II*, which is derived from the accounts by Hall and Holinshed of these events.

The succeeding plays, *Henry IV, Parts 1 and 2*, take up the principal historical facts about the reign of Henry IV shortly after his accession, a reign disfigured by numerous conspiracies and rebellions. Most of these turmoils, like the revolt of the Percy family, who were dissatisfied with the recognition accorded their services in securing Henry's throne, resulted from Henry's own earlier rebellion. Henry succeeded in overcoming all these assaults, but his illness in his last years and his poor financial skills made his inheritance difficult for his son, who became Henry V.

Historians agree that as Prince of Wales Henry V had indeed displayed valor of the kind shown in *Henry IV, Part 1*. He probably did not personally fight Hotspur at Shrewsbury as he does in the play, but he did lead the King's army. Though the Prince had political differences with his father, most of the stories about his misspent youth, particularly that of his striking the Lord Chief Justice for punishing one of the Prince's companions, are now felt to be merely hearsay, preserved by such chroniclers as John Stow (from whom Shakespeare borrowed a few phrases, and the idea of the Prince reimbursing the victims of his depredations). In numerous campaigns the historical Henry V proved a daring and intelligent young man of considerable political and military prowess long before he became King, and his reign itself, widely regarded as one of the most brilliant phases of English history, was of particular interest to the Tudor dynasty, as will be seen below. Henry's abrupt death, however, and his many wars, left a poor legacy to his infant son, whose disastrous reign is the subject of most of Shakespeare's first tetralogy (the three parts of *Henry VI*, and *Richard III*).

THE THEATRICAL BACKGROUND

The Elizabethan stage and its conventions represent one of the most flexible and diversified theaters in the history of drama. It can be considered circumscribed only in the matter of scenery, and this limitation proved advantageous for swift scene changes and cross-cutting of the action as well as for poetic creation of locale and atmosphere, such as we get in the opening flourish of the King's entry in *Henry IV, Part 1*, or in the description of the weather at the beginning of Act V. The diversity and range of the Elizabethan stage in all other respects derives from its complex origins.

The first and most ancient forerunner of the Elizabethan play is the pagan festival, going back to classical times, which survived in a submerged form throughout the Christian period of the Middle Ages (and in some cases, like certain of the Christmas, New Year, and Easter traditions, to the present day). The festivals persisted partly because the Catholic church decided not to abolish the old forms so much as to rededicate them to Christian purposes. The prominence of this strain in Shakespeare's theater is shown in his own frequent use of such festival occasions, as in *A Midsummer Night's Dream* (which also includes May Day material), *Twelfth Night*, and the woodland rites of *The Merry Wives of Windsor*. The placing of Sir John Falstaff as the central figure in this latter non-Christian ritual should remind us that he maintains the amoral pagan tradition in his role in the history plays also. Many of the pagan festivals were occasions for emotional release, a release often symptomized by reversals of conventional values. Such figures as the Lord of Misrule and the Boy Bishop temporarily usurped authority—sometimes to the scandal of the church. (Probably, modern beauty "queens," and certainly the *Rex* of the New Orleans Mardi Gras, are modern survivals.) Falstaff usurps authority somewhat similarly when he plays the King in Act II, scene iv, of *Henry IV, Part 1;* and throughout the play he reverses conventional values, seeking to turn the future reign of Prince Hal into a veritable Kingdom of Misrule.

Throughout the Middle Ages, simultaneous with the pagan survivals and sometimes mingled with them, an orthodox Christian tradition of drama was evolving. The mass itself is often called a ritual drama, and it readily encouraged semidramatic interpolations (called "tropes") to illustrate episodes from the Bible and the life of Christ in particular. Such episodes eventually accumulated to provide a kind of continuous sequence of dramatized scripture, and it became customary to perform them together to celebrate Corpus Christi Day—a day in late May or June, and hence one of the year's longest, and more likely to bring fine summer weather for outdoor performances. Numerous such cycles existed in England, at Coventry and Wakefield, for instance; and some of these "mystery plays" have since been revived, as at Chester and York. Although the intent of the term "mystery play" is debated, the name is appropriate because these dramatic cycles dealt with religious history from the Creation to the Last Judgment, and thus with the central Christian mysteries. Later, the theme of religious history naturally suggested the inclusion of postbiblical matter, particularly the histories of the saints, which often followed patterns suggested by the miraculous happenings of the lives of Christ and the Apostles. This kind of "miracle" play was particularly popular in France, and was usually performed on the day sacred to the saint (for example, the *Play of St. Nicholas*).

Both these styles of play survived into the age of Shakespeare. He may well have seen the last performance of the Coventry plays, which were staged in some form as late as 1585 within walking distance of Stratford; traces of miracle-play motifs appear in Shakespeare's early history plays, in scenes dealing with Saint Joan (naturally an unsympathetic figure to the English) and with the saintly Henry VI, Hal's son. The metaphysical imagery so marked in Falstaff's speech reflects this religious inheritance, as do all the numerous allusions to heaven, hell, angels, devils, and the like, both in the history plays and in the major tragedies —*Othello*, for one. However, by the time Shakespeare lived the medieval plays were unfashionable—they were both ancient and tinged with "papist" associations. More popular were the moralizing dramas that developed in the late fifteenth century, whose characters were allegorical figures usually grouped round a central human figure, such as Mankind in *The Castle of Perseverance*. The Protestant concern with ethics delighted in the interplay, about such a figure, of personifications like Lust, Folly, Gluttony, and Sloth on the one hand, and Chastity, Industry, and Generosity, on the other. The vices (like the earlier devils of the mysteries) often have the most vigorous lines; and this tradition was enormously popular in sixteenth-century England. Such plays as *Everyman*, *Mankind*, and *Wit and Science* clearly lead directly toward first Marlowe's *Dr. Faustus*, with its good and bad angels, and then *Henry IV, Part 1*, with its youthful Prince tempted alternately by "a devil that haunts thee in the likeness of an old fat man . . . that reverend Vice, that grey Iniquity," and by the rash pride and lust for honor of Hotspur. The Lord Chief Justice of the second part is another of these now more delicately psychologized morality figures, putting pressure on Hal.

This "morality" tradition evolved markedly under the influence of the Tudors in the earlier sixteenth century. Morality plays like Skelton's *Magnificence* stressed political themes, and throughout the century the attitude toward history in general reflected this moralizing tendency. It appears in one of the most famous collections of narratives of the period, *The Mirror for Magistrates* (1559), to the various editions of which many authors contributed, among them Thomas Sackville (co-author of the earliest English tragedy, *Gorboduc*). History is treated here as a series of exemplary episodes for the study of rulers, and many of the most popular figures of past ages appear in the anthology, including several, such as Richard II and King Lear, with whom Shakespeare would later deal.

The moralizing purpose of Elizabethan historical writing remained prominent in Shakespeare's favorite historical sources, the far more elaborate and more plausible chronicles of British history written by Edward Hall and Raphael Holinshed; in particular, the stark moralism of Hall is characteristic of Shakespeare's earlier cycle, that dealing with Henry VI. The Elizabethan chroniclers also reflect the increasing political awareness that the Tudor dynasty stimulated on behalf of its nationalistic and anti-papal policy. The comparatively remote claims of the Tudors to the succession encouraged them to have history rewritten to vindicate their possession of the crown. Polydore Vergil, an Italian humanist, was employed to reinterpret the past to suit the Tudor present; and the *History of Richard III*, attributed to Sir Thomas More, was a highly moralistic but also very politically slanted account of the supposed depravity and deformity of the last Yorkist monarch, who was overthrown and killed by the first Tudor king, Henry VII.

Of more immediate interest to us is the way in which, particularly after Elizabeth's accession, the theater began to reflect these political tendencies by presenting chronicle plays devoted to appropriate phases, mythical or otherwise, of English history. The analogy to Tudor policies that might be found, for example, in the reign of King John (who was excommunicated for defying the papal authority) had already by 1540 encouraged Bishop John Bale to devote a kind of morality play to the subject of that monarch. This anti-papal play illustrates polemical views that may be traced down to Shakespeare's own play *King John*. It is clear also, however, that Shakespeare is less and less interested in following

a particular "line" in this and in later plays than by the compli-
cation of motives and complexity of interpretation that the various political and moral cross-currents of the Tudor period projected into the historical past, thus leaving him a wide variety of
interpretations to draw upon. The Tudors naturally found the
Lancastrian kings of interest as models for a new dynasty with
limited claims to the succession; for, most conspicuously in
Henry V, the Lancastrians had shown a capacity to command the
loyal enthusiasm of all Englishmen in a series of dazzling military exploits against the French. For the highly intellectual Tudors, the education and background of this brilliant prince would
be of the greatest interest, as appears in the extended accounts of
him in the chronicles of Hall and Holinshed. This kind of concern was readily extended beyond politics to questions of ethics
and manners, as we see in such models for Shakespeare's version
of Prince Hal as John Lyly's study, in his play *Campaspe*, of the
youthful Alexander's emotional maturing.

In general, the aristocratic wit and comedy of John Lyly, with
its marked verbal play and puns, offer Shakespeare some suggestions for the verbal virtuosity of the exchanges between Falstaff
and Hal (see Act I, scene ii, for examples). In many such ways the
whole sequence from *Richard II* to *Henry V* is deeply saturated
in the aristocratic life and interests of the Tudor courts. Elizabeth
herself supposedly ordered another "Falstaff" play from Shakespeare, after the two parts of *Henry IV*, and he then produced
The Merry Wives of Windsor. Later the Earl of Essex found the
deposition of Richard II as relevant to his plans for seizing the
succession as the Tudors had found it to theirs, and Essex had
Shakespeare's play performed as a prelude to his rebellion aimed
at deposing Elizabeth in 1601.

Closely allied to the aristocratic elements in the Elizabethan
theater were the consequences of the strong association of the
universities with sixteenth-century drama. The earliest English
tragedy, *Gorboduc*, shared the political intent of the later history
plays, studying problems of succession. It was performed, perhaps with conscious admonition, before the unmarried, heirless
Queen Elizabeth at Whitehall in 1562, by the law students of the

Inns of Court in London. Like much later Elizabethan drama of an academic kind, it was modeled on classical drama, and particularly on the plays of Seneca. Many of the characteristics of Senecan tragedy—murders, ghosts, madness, revenge—reappear in many Elizabethan plays, among them Kyd's *Spanish Tragedy* and Shakespeare's *Hamlet*. Such authors as Thomas Kyd, and Christopher Marlowe in a play like his *Edward II*, also illustrate the strong influence of graduates of Cambridge and Oxford on the literary resources of the Elizabethan theater. It is in part from them that Shakespeare derives his sense of the medieval tragic rhythm, the wheel of fortune, best illustrated in Lydgate's narrative, *The Fall of Princes* (1494). *Henry IV, Part 1*, in the career of Hotspur, shares in this tradition; but the tradition appears even more clearly in the preceding play, in the downfall of Richard II. The lighter academic tradition, that of classical and Italian comedy and of the mime, is not markedly present in *Henry IV, Part 1*, but the spirited influence of university men like Robert Greene and Thomas Lodge appears in some of Shakespeare's comedies—*As you Like It*, for one—and his women (including, perhaps, Lady Percy) derive some of their charm from these vivacious sources.

However, the theater in England was fortunate in not being exclusively aristocratic and academic. Neither of its two greatest authors, Shakespeare and Ben Jonson, was a graduate of a university, though both had excellent secondary schooling. And the tradition of the Elizabethan theatrical companies was essentially practical; in their latest form they were definitely commercial enterprises, as is evident from the diaries kept by one of the major theatrical entrepreneurs of the period, Philip Henslowe. As we have seen, the twin roots of the companies were the clerical and secular medieval festivals. The former were obviously handled initially by the clergy; the latter, by laymen. As the religious drama became progressively secularized, the clergy's role in it was taken over by citizens, in particular by the trade guilds of craftsmen—a fact recalled by the tradesmen's play in *A Midsummer Night's Dream*. Their scenery was limited and, as performances frequently were duplicated in various parts of a town, it was natural to mount each episode on a large flat wagon that would move progressively from one scheduled place of performance to the next. Inevitably, the success of these dramas encouraged the emergence of more or less professional actors, who found it possible to establish a career by traveling from town to town throughout the year. Performances were held in aristocrats' palace halls, or in such convenient spots as the yards of inns.

Each of these locales has a bearing on Shakespearean drama—but the impact of inn yards as a *venue* is more readily identifiable. Inns were built in a hollow square, with access to the rooms on the inside wall given by open stairs and galleries. These made a natural vantage point for spectators, and access to the yard was readily controlled at the single carriage entrance. The stage was built against one wall, which meant that above it were to be found two or three galleries—useful for the variation of acting levels (as in the balcony scene of *Romeo and Juliet*) or for musicians. Beneath the lower gallery would be a kind of "inner stage," which could be curtained off for scene changes or used for concealment (as when Falstaff hides from the watch in Act II, scene iv). Behind this in turn could lie the normal line of inn rooms, some of which would be used as changing rooms and the like by the players. This is the basic structure of the Elizabethan public theaters; but the first model for these, James Burbage's Theatre (built outside the city limits, at Shoreditch, by 1576), was round in shape, like the rings used for bearbaiting and bullbaiting, for which it may also have served. The pattern was duplicated shortly afterward by Philip Henslowe with the Curtain playhouse, and later came the Rose, which he built at Bankside, across the river from the Curtain. Burbage's sons tore down the Theatre because of troubles with land leases and rebuilt it as the Globe at Bankside in 1599. All these playhouses followed the same structure, one also reflected to some degree in modern theatrical audience arrangement, although in Elizabethan times the audience stood around the stage, and sat in the galleries, which were considered the better places. The effect resembled that of modern performances on an "open stage" and was obviously different from the twentieth-century picture-frame effect of the proscenium arch.

The stage projected into the audience, whose members stood around it on three sides and were even sometimes allowed to sit on it, for a price. Thus, the relations of actor and audience were intimate and informal, and asides and soliloquies like Hal's and Falstaff's seemed quite natural. All inn yards and many early theaters (like the Globe), however, were unroofed and exposed to daylight, though a canopy might protect the stage. This lack of a roof encouraged rhetorical manner (as in the "King Cambyses vein" mentioned in II.iv.329), and a high-pitched poetic style such as Hotspur often favors. The King's solemn opening speech would have to dominate an unruly audience in an uncovered enclosure—hence its formality and rhetorical emphasis. Scenery too would be lacking. This lack would be offset by careful verbal scene settings (see the "night" scenes of Act II), by elaborate costuming (note the gorgeous descriptions of the warriors' armor at the battle of Shrewsbury), and by vigorous movement—the early traveling companies had to diversify their resources with wrestling (as in *As You Like It*), with dancing (as in most of the comedies), and with fencing and sword fights (as in *Hamlet* and the battle scenes in *Henry IV*). The actors would be practiced swordsmen and acrobats, and the fights would not be the tame affairs modern actors put on all too often.

These skilled entertainers who made up the theatrical companies lived in precarious conditions in the early years of Elizabeth's reign. Actors, as itinerant, "masterless" men, could be prosecuted as vagrants by law from 1572, unless they could show that they were formally members of a noble household. Even the possession of an aristocratic patron left the companies exposed to the hatred of the often puritan middle classes, who regarded the theaters as disreputable incitements to indolence or riot. The urban authorities, particularly the Council of the City of London, harassed the players on moral and administrative grounds. Plausibly enough, they usually closed the theaters when plague broke out (as in the disastrous period from 1592 to 1594), as places whence the disease might be disseminated. The general resistance of the City had from the start normally obliged the companies to establish their new permanent theaters outside its jurisdiction,

Changling
Simpleton
French Dancing Mr
Falſtafe
Hoſtes
Clauſe

Courtesy of the Huntington Library

Frontispiece from *The Wits* (see p. 171). The figures of Falstaff and Mrs. Quickly are in the left foreground; the others are from Jacobean plays. The theater is a private, indoor one, keeping the projecting stage.

either in the suburbs, where the Theatre was built, or across the Thames on the south bank, where the Globe stood. The interest of the Queen and the Court, before whom they regularly performed, gave the companies enough protection to survive in such surroundings and, until the plague of 1592, there existed quite a number of companies with aristocratic patrons (as well as two boys' groups, associated with schools within the City). Sometime before 1592, Shakespeare appears likely to have joined some such company; and in 1594 he was certainly a member of the Lord Chamberlain's company. The Lord Chamberlain was an important dignitary who controlled the court entertainments; and the official character of his theatrical company was further enhanced when it received from James I the title of the King's Men, an honor involving some status in the court. The early history of this company and of its members, including Shakespeare, remains in many ways uncertain and conjectural, but after 1594 it achieved stability and prospered—to Shakespeare's advantage and to that of Richard Burbage, its principal actor. Only one other company survived to rival it significantly—the Lord Admiral's Men, who used Henslowe's theaters.

Even in their most flourishing state, however, Elizabethan theatrical companies were not remunerative to their authors and actors, as such. Shakespeare and Burbage prospered as shareholders in their company and were unusual in making fortunes in the theater (like Henslowe and Alleyn in their rival company). Unless they were academic or aristocratic amateurs, most men of the theater, particularly before 1594, lived in penury, like Robert Greene, or took other jobs, like Christopher Marlowe's police-spying. Even rather later, a prominent author like Ben Jonson depended greatly on rather precarious aristocratic patronage, which ultimately failed Jonson. (A very full account of the complex material about the theatrical companies appears in the various studies by E. K. Chambers listed in Appendix E.)

SHAKESPEARE'S COMPOSITION OF HENRY IV

When, probably at some time in 1596, he turned his attention to the reign of Henry IV, Shakespeare had reached his artistic maturity. Five years earlier he had developed his skill in revising the older *Henry VI* history plays. He had then reached an early formal perfection in *Richard III*; but he had shown himself also a consummate master both of comedy (in such a deftly written play as *A Midsummer Night's Dream*) and of tragedy (in the romantic mood, with *Romeo and Juliet*). In *Richard II*, the play preceding *Henry IV*, he had evinced a more profound and subtle concern for political issues than in his earlier plays and had fused them with a brilliant and near-tragic theme in the fall of the fascinating figure of Richard. Now, with *Henry IV*, Shakespeare was ingeniously to unite the world of politics with the humor of his comedies, to their mutual enhancement.

The choice of subject in the second tetralogy was governed by the interest, for Shakespeare's era of fervent, Protestant, English nationalism, that lay in the reign of Henry V with its triumphant successes in France, which seemed an inevitable comparison for the age of Elizabeth with its defeat of the Spanish Armada in 1588. Further, the uncertainty about who would succeed Queen Elizabeth made Englishmen particularly interested in the nature of hereditary succession and its alternatives. In immediate practical terms, this interest reached its climax in the Earl of Essex's conspiracy to depose Elizabeth and himself ascend the throne (an act for which he used the precedent of Shakespeare's treatment of the earlier career of Henry IV); and there were also many more speculative literary studies of the problem of succession, beginning with the first English tragedy, *Gorboduc* (performed before Elizabeth in 1562), and extending to *Macbeth* and *King Lear*. A related but more positive theme that clearly concerned Shakespeare (as well as his age) was the nature of the ideal ruler—of which Henry V was a conspicuous example (though Shakespeare's view of Henry is by no means unequivocal). The impact of distorted versions of Machiavelli's *The Prince* (an authentic translation of which was not published until 1640) had made this question of great interest to Englishmen, who were inclined to conceive a successful politician in the Machiavellian mode to be, like Shakespeare's Richard III, scarcely less than diabolic. Shakespeare may well have conceived his characterization of Henry IV with a now more discriminating sense of Machiavelli's views in mind; but his principal concern was, of course, with the evolution of Prince Hal from an adolescent nonconformist to an effective though not infallible sovereign.

Shakespeare would recognize discussion of all these themes latent in the story of the reigns of Richard and the Henries, not only because he found a highly moralistic account of them in such narratives as Holinshed's history of Great Britain, but also because they had already caught popular interest in the guise of several anonymous minor plays, particularly one called *The Famous Victories of Henry V*, a version of which was performed at least as early as 1588. There was also a precedent for a more elevated literary treatment in Samuel Daniel's *The Civil Wars Between the Two Houses of Lancaster and York* (1595), which Shakespeare certainly drew on for some details (see Appendix B for a detailed discussion of this and other debts). The epic nationalism of the border battles between the English Percy family and such Scots noblemen as the Earl of Douglas were also celebrated in widely popular ballads like *The Hunting of the Cheviot*, in which Hotspur and Douglas figure prominently.

Shakespeare's most individual contribution to his raw material probably lies in his development of the figure of Falstaff, though he may well have found suggestions for his comic scenes not only in the comic scenes of *The Famous Victories* but also in an anonymous play, *Woodstock* (*ca.* 1591), which may also have helped him in writing *Richard II*. A. R. Humphreys notes that in *Woodstock*, which also deals with Richard's reign, a corrupt Lord Chief Justice fosters anarchy in the kingdom by organizing a gang of robbers like those in *Henry IV*. This figure addresses his victims in terms similar to those of Falstaff at the Gadshill robbery, shows similar adroitness in managing his affairs, and prides himself on the fact that with his appointment he is "sweld more plump." The bearing of this theme on the main political action is similar to Falstaff's in *Henry IV*.

It is usually assumed that our text of *Henry IV* represents at least one major revision of Shakespeare's first version, if not more; but, whatever the exact relationship of the text to earlier versions, Shakespearean or otherwise, it is certain that the development of the comic role of Falstaff under his original name of Sir John Oldcastle (see an unexcised allusion in "my old lad of the castle," Act I, scene ii, line 37) caused great popular interest and some indignation. The name and role of Oldcastle had figured without distinction in *The Famous Victories*, but his new prominence and extravagance of character offended the historical Oldcastle's descendants, particularly the Brooke family, headed by the Lords Cobham. The original Oldcastle had been a soldier of merit noted for his leadership of the Lollard group of church reformers, for which he died a martyr in 1417. He was known as "the good Lord Cobham," from his marriage to the heiress of Lord Cobham in 1408. At first a friend of Prince Hal, he later rebelled as a result of religious persecution.

Perhaps thinking of the cowardice he had (mistakenly) ascribed to the historical Sir John Fastolfe in the first part of *Henry VI* (IV.i), Shakespeare hastily met the protests of the Brooke family by substituting the only slightly distorted name of Sir John Falstaff for that of Oldcastle, leaving as a result all kinds of minor irregularities both of metrics (see II.ii.91) and of history (Fastolfe actually died in Henry VI's reign, not in Henry V's as Shakespeare has it in *Henry V*). The slights on Fastolfe are scarcely more deserved than those on Oldcastle: Fastolfe appears to have been a tough, responsible, and efficient soldier, highly esteemed but mean and ambitious. His "retreat" at the battle of Patay seems unlikely to have been cowardice; he was knighted for bravery at Agincourt and continued to hold high positions thereafter. Traces of the historical Oldcastle and Fastolfe can be found respectively in the theology and (ironic) canting style of Falstaff, and in a certain financial meanness, but the character of Shakespeare's figure and his influence on Hal depend on a vast range of other resources, including the vice figures and the allegorical debates of the morality plays, as already mentioned.

THE NATURE OF THE TEXT

The Elizabethan dramatist customarily sold his manuscript and all his rights in it directly to the players for a cash payment. Often, the manuscript would be inadequately prepared for theatrical production—it would not have a standard format, and it would lack stage directions and exact conformity to the requirements of staging. The players would then correct the manuscript to make a prompt copy, either directly from the author's script or from a new, emended scribal copy. In turn actors' parts would be prepared, carrying only the cues and lines for each role. The plays were not normally printed until their value for performance was considerably diminished or until the company fell into difficulties financially, as during the suspension of performances in a plague year. However, many circumstances did hasten publication—in particular, surreptitious publication of a "pirated" text by unscrupulous printers, who either stole scripts, hired stenographers to write down the text from performances, or bribed actors to dictate their parts and what they could remember of the rest of the play. Such texts are poor, inevitably, and are called "bad quartos" (a quarto being a book made of paper sheets of a standard fifteen-by-ten-inch size, each of which was folded twice to make four book leaves—a format better suited to small editions of single plays than the larger "folios," which were folded only once and usually printed in double columns).

When an authorized publication was made, the text was sold to a printer by the players and was officially recorded by him in the register of the Stationers' Company. This text was not necessarily that originally provided by the author; it might be a prompt-book with director's revisions, or even, as the text of *Macbeth* probably was, a rewritten version. The first and the only authoritative collected edition of Shakespeare's plays is the First Folio of 1623, prepared by Shakespeare's fellow actors

Heminges and Condell (references to it are abbreviated to F in this edition). It depends on a wide variety of such types of source and on some of the nineteen earlier, published quartos of the thirty-six plays it included (only *Pericles* has since been added to these, as Shakespeare's). However, in the case of the first quarto of *Henry IV, Part 1* (dated 1598) the limited stage directions and lack of director's correction of unsatisfactory exits and entrances (for example, at the beginning of Act II, scene ii; see note on page 37) suggest that the printer's source was either the author's copy or, possibly, a fair copy of it, since more regularity occurs in the forms of the speakers' names than is usual in an author's copy (such as the play's second part). It has been plausibly suggested by A. R. Humphreys that this standardization might result from Shakespeare's own corrections, arising from the trouble with the Oldcastle family over Falstaff's earlier name, Sir John Oldcastle. The dramatically sound punctuation, the metrical precision of the elision (or lack of it) in the weak verb ending (-*ed*), and certain colloquial touches that transcribers often "correct" all suggest we are dealing in the first quarto with Shakespeare's own version, obscured only by compositors' minor errors and "improvements." No emendations made in the later quartos and the folio collected editions suggest that they have a more authoritative source than the first quarto itself; the changes are all minor and are such as an editor or a compositor might make. An extant four-leaved fragment of a quarto (used in binding a copy of an Elizabethan grammar book) shows that a lost first quarto edition existed, but the fragment is similar to the first fully available quarto.

An editor, therefore, will naturally choose to base an edition of *Henry IV, Part 1*, on the text of the first quarto, which is followed here, as it has been by nearly all modern editions since the Cambridge edition of 1863. This Cambridge text (now available in the Macmillan Globe edition) was edited by W. G. Clark and W. A. Wright. It "practically settled the major textual problems of the play, and has been followed by most editors since," according to the Variorum Edition by S. B. Hemingway (1936). The original Cambridge edition is the model for the present edition,

hot as molten lead,& as heauie too:God keepe leade out of me,
I need no more weight then mine owne bowels. I haue led my
rag of Muffins where they are pepperd,theres not three of my
150.left aliue, and they are for the townes ende, to beg during
life:but who comes here?   *Enter the Prince.*

Prin. What, stands thou idle here?lend me thy sword,
Many a noble man lies starke and stiffe,
Vnder the hoofes of vaunting enemies,
whose deaths are yet vnreuengd,I preethe lend mee thy sword.

*Falst.*O Hal,*I* preethe giue me leaue to breath a while,Turke
Gregorie neuer did such deeds in armes as I haue don this day,
I haue paid Percy,I haue made him sure.

Prin, He is indeed,and liuing to kill thee :
I preethe lend me thy sword.

Fal, Nay before God Hal,if Percy be aliue thou gets not my
sword,but take my pistoll if thou wilt.

Prin. Giue it me,what ? is it in the case ?

Falst. I Hal,tis hot,tis hot,theres that will sacke a Citie.
The Prince drawes it out,and finds it to be a bottle of Sacke.

Prin. What is it a time to iest and dally now?
          He throwes the bottle at him,   *Exit,*

Falst. Well if Percy be aliue,ile pierce him;if hee doe come in
my way so,if he doe not,if *I* come in his willingly,let him make
a Carbonado of me. I like not such grinning honour as sir Walter hath,giue me life,which if I can saue,so : if not, honor comes
vnlookt for,and theres an end.

Alarme,excursions,Enter the King,the Prince,Lord Iohn
of Lancaster, Earle of Westmorland.

King. I preethe Harry withdraw thy selfe,thou bleedest too
Lord Iohn of Lancaster go you with him.   (much,

P.Iohn. Not I my Lord,vnlesse I did bleed too.

Prin. Ibeseech your maiestie make vp,
Least your retirement do amaze your friends.   (tent.

King. I will do so.My Lord of Westmerland lead him to his
West. Come my Lord,ile lead you to your tent.

Prin. Lead me my Lord? I do not need your helpe,
And God forbid a shallow scratch should driue

                                             The

A typical page (sig K1v.) from the first Quarto (1598)—compare this with
pages 143–5 (V.iii.33–V.iv.10.)

XXV

but it has been carefully revised and collated with the New Variorum, New Cambridge, Alexander, and New Arden editions, among others, as well as checked against the British Museum first quarto (referred to as Q1 in this edition). As this 1598 text of the play is close to Shakespeare's own version, the present edition, like most modern ones, seeks to avoid serious deviations from it and notes any changes that have been made. However, the present text differs considerably from many modern commercial editions that preserve the accretions contributed to the original text by generations of editors. Nicholas Rowe's 1709 edition was the first modern one; it and that of Edward Capell have had the most persistent, and often the most pernicious, influence. All their work has been cleared away (Rowe's unhelpful list of characters, for example, and Capell's dubious stage directions), except where modern scholarship has vindicated them. The few original quarto directions have been preserved, except where they are unclear, and then any changes are indicated. All other stage directions have been revised, reformed, and extended wherever necessary or helpful to the reader. For example, neither time nor place were indicated in the quarto, and I have added these according to the indications in the speeches. All such new stage directions (often abbreviated in the notes to S.D.) are enclosed by square brackets. The act and scene divisions, added in the first collected folio edition of Shakespeare in 1623, are preserved to facilitate reference but are given within brackets because they almost certainly have no bearing on the play's original unbroken performance.

The punctuation in the text given here differs somewhat from that of the Cambridge edition. I have kept it as close to the original as consistency and clarity for the modern reader would allow. That is to say that the pointing is rather more rhetorical than syntactical, in so far as this does not misleadingly conflict with modern usage. Thus, rather than marking the formal grammatical structure of clauses, phrases, and the like, the punctuation merely indicates the actor's natural pauses for breath and emphasis, to augment freedom of movement in reading the text. Such awkwardnesses as the excessive use of commas and colons in the quarto have not been adhered to, however, where for example this produces a sentence which a modern mind expects to find as two or three separate sentences, or where phrase or clause relationships become unclear. Further, I have freely substituted dashes for commas to clarify clause structure. Any such changes in the text's punctuation are recorded in the notes only when they change the apparent meaning of the original.

Spelling has been thoroughly modernized throughout the volume and generally conforms to modern pronunciation, except where accents or footnotes indicate otherwise (but see also the appendix on Elizabethan English). The Folio's and any other later texts' variant readings from the quarto are usually recorded only when they are adopted in the text. The most frequent problem of format, relineation of irregular verse, is noted only in significant cases, as it usually involves no substantive changes. Finally, it may be noted that I have preserved (and extended, where consistency required it) the capitalization of the first letter of all personifications, allegorical abstractions, invented titles, and the like, to which a sustained pattern of allusion occurs (see Falstaff's speech, I.ii.20–26). This usually clarifies the status of such terms and the function of the figures of speech dependent on them. Typical examples are Hal's allusions to the morality play Vices: Iniquity, Vanity, and so on (II.iv.386ff.). On the other hand, ranks and honorific terms ("my lord," "your grace") are given an initial capital only when they appear as part of a specific title ("my Lord of Westmoreland").

All references to and quotations from other works of Shakespeare follow the text and lineation of the *Tudor Shakespeare*, edited by Peter Alexander (London, 1951). Editors who have contributed much to the play are referred to in the commentary and elsewhere by name only, as Rowe, Pope, Theobald, Malone. A full dated list of major editions may easily be found in volumes of the *New Variorum Shakespeare*, among the appendixes to each play; or see E. K. Chambers, *William Shakespeare* (Oxford, 1930), Volume I, pages 275-277. These lists do not include such important recent one-volume editions of Shakespeare's works as those of G. L. Kittredge (1936), Peter Alexander (1951), and C. J. Sisson (1954).

The English Royal Family from EDWARD III 1312–1377 to Shakespeare's time

(only names mentioned in Henry IV, Part I, or significant in the line of descent, are given.)

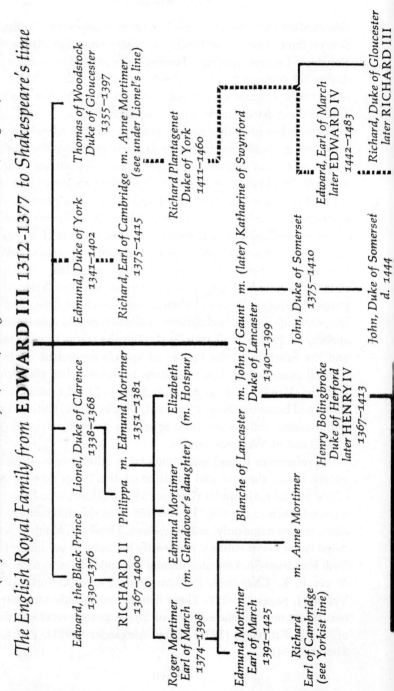

Edward, the Black Prince 1330–1376

Lionel, Duke of Clarence 1338–1368

Edmund, Duke of York 1341–1402

Thomas of Woodstock Duke of Gloucester 1355–1397

RICHARD II 1367–1400 o

Philippa m. Edmund Mortimer 1351–1381

Richard, Earl of Cambridge 1375–1415

m. Anne Mortimer (see under Lionel's line)

Edmund Mortimer (m. Glendower's daughter)

Elizabeth (m. Hotspur)

Richard Plantagenet Duke of York 1411–1460

Roger Mortimer Earl of March 1374–1398

Blanche of Lancaster m. John of Gaunt Duke of Lancaster 1340–1399

m. (later) Katharine of Swynford

Edward, Earl of March later EDWARD IV 1442–1483

Richard, Duke of Gloucester later RICHARD III

Edmund Mortimer Earl of March 1391–1425

m. Anne Mortimer

Henry Bolingbroke Duke of Herford later HENRY IV 1367–1413

John, Duke of Somerset 1375–1410

Richard Earl of Cambridge (see Yorkist line)

John, Duke of Somerset d. 1444

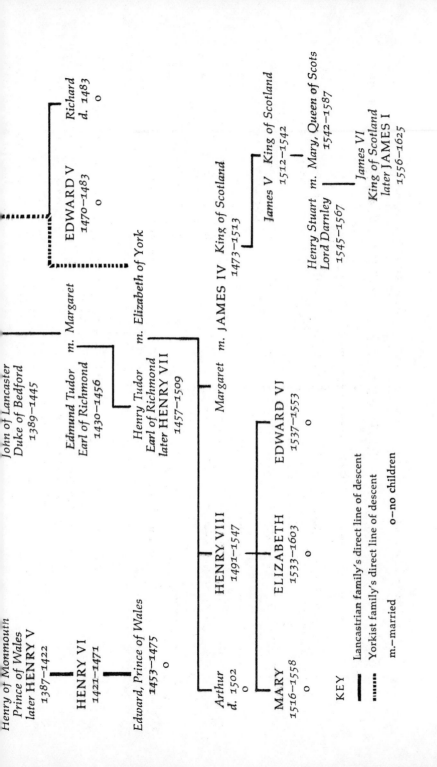

Henry of Monmouth
Prince of Wales
later HENRY V
1387–1422

HENRY VI
1421–1471

Edward, Prince of Wales
1453–1475
o

John of Lancaster
Duke of Bedford
1389–1445

Edward V
1470–1483
o

Richard
d. 1483
o

Edmund Tudor
Earl of Richmond
1430–1456
m. Margaret

Henry Tudor
Earl of Richmond
later HENRY VII
1457–1509
m. Elizabeth of York

Margaret   m.   JAMES IV   King of Scotland
1473–1513

James V   King of Scotland
1512–1542

Henry Stuart   m.   Mary, Queen of Scots
Lord Darnley   1542–1587
1545–1567

James VI
King of Scotland
later JAMES I
1556–1625

Arthur
d. 1502
o

HENRY VIII
1491–1547

MARY
1516–1558
o

ELIZABETH
1533–1603
o

EDWARD VI
1537–1553
o

KEY

—— Lancastrian family's direct line of descent

······ Yorkist family's direct line of descent

m.–married   o–no children

CHARACTERS*

KING HENRY THE FOURTH *son of John of Gaunt and first cousin to Richard the Second (whom he dethroned); called Henry Bolingbroke, Duke of Hereford, before becoming King.*

HENRY, PRINCE OF WALES *eldest son and heir to the King; familiarly called Hal.*

LORD JOHN OF LANCASTER *younger brother to the Prince.*

EARL OF WESTMORELAND *adviser to King Henry.*

SIR WALTER BLUNT *personal attendant to the King.*

HENRY PERCY *Earl of Northumberland, major supporter of Henry in his revolt against Richard the Second.*

THOMAS PERCY *Earl of Worcester (pronounced woōs'ter), brother to the Earl of Northumberland.*

HENRY PERCY *customarily called Hotspur, son of the Earl of Northumberland; supposed in the play to be of comparable age to the Prince of Wales, but historically much older.*

EDMUND MORTIMER *Earl of March. In the play he shares the attributes of two historical members of his family, both bearing this name: one was named heir to Richard the Second, and the other was the fellow rebel and son-in-law of Glendower. (See I.iii.83, note.)*

ARCHIBALD *Earl of Douglas, a Scots general.*

OWEN GLENDOWER *a Welsh rebel cultivating traditional Celtic lore.*

SIR RICHARD VERNON *an ally of the Percy family.*

RICHARD SCROOP *Archbishop of York, sympathetic to the rebels against King Henry.*

SIR MICHAEL *a friend of the Archbishop; the "Sir" here probably denotes a priest with a bachelor's degree, not the knightly title.*

SIR JOHN FALSTAFF *a largely fictional character who, before winning knighthood, was supposedly a page to the Duke of Norfolk. His historical prototypes (Sir John Oldcastle and Sir John Fastolfe) were men of courage and moral stature who are not necessarily to be closely identified with him.*

NED POINS *a quick-witted commoner.*

---

* By the present editor. No list of *dramatis personae* appears in either Qq or F; the first editor to supply such lists was Nicholas Rowe, in 1709.

PETO   *a hanger-on of Falstaff.*

BARDOLPH   *a drunken follower of Falstaff.*

GADSHILL   *a highwayman (named after a place famous for hold-ups).*

FRANCIS   *a servingman.*

LADY PERCY   *wife of Hotspur and sister to Mortimer; here familiarly called Kate, though historically she was called Elizabeth.*

LADY MORTIMER   *Mortimer's Welsh wife, daughter of Glendower.*

MISTRESS QUICKLY   *hostess of the Boar's Head Tavern in Eastcheap, London.*

Various aristocrats, officials, servants, travellers, and soldiers.

Time and Place

The play begins in the year 1402 and is set in various parts of England and Wales.

The only authentic indications of time and place in Shakespeare's plays are those given in the speeches of the characters. For the convenience of the modern reader, however, time and place indications have been supplied in this edition, enclosed in square brackets to show their lack of textual authority. As regards time it should be noted that, until the battle of Shrewsbury, there are three fairly independent (but ingeniously interwoven) temporal sequences of scenes. The Falstaff scenes in Acts I to IV follow on from each other very closely, but they alternate with scenes presenting the activities of the King and rebels between which weeks and even months may have elapsed.

The First Part of the History
of King Henry the Fourth

[*Act I, scene i: London, the King's Palace. September, A.D.
1402.*] *Enter the* KING, LORD JOHN OF LANCASTER, EARL OF WEST-
MORELAND, [SIR WALTER BLUNT,] *with others.*

KING

So shaken as we are, so wan with care,
Find we a time for frighted peace to pant,
And breathe short-winded accents of new broils
To be commenced in strands afar remote:
5   No more the thirsty entrance of this soil,
Shall daub her lips with her own children's blood,

The First . . . Fourth   Qq read: The Historie of Henry the fourth.
Act I, scene i   F has *Actus Primus. Scaena Prima.* There are no act
or scene divisions in Qq; these divisions appear in Latin throughout F
and have been translated without footnote in all later scenes of this
text.
London. The King's Palace. September, A.D. 1402   No locations or
times are given in the early texts; all these in later scenes have been
added or revised by the present editor on the basis of internal evidence
or of Shakespeare's historical sources, without further notation. See
the Note on Time and Place below the List of Characters.
Enter . . . others   Sir Walter Blunt is not listed by QqF; perhaps he
entered later.
    1. *shaken*   The previous play, *RII*, ended with disorders resulting
from Henry's accession.
    4. *strands*   stronds Qq; such minor phonetic eccentricities as
"stronds" are modernized hereafter, usually without note.
    5–6. *thirsty . . . blood*   Malone cites God's words to Cain after the
murder of Abel, Genesis 4:11: "Now therefore thou art cursed from
the earth, which hath opened her mouth to receive thy brother's blood
from thine hand." *thirsty entrance*   absorbent surface.

1

No more shall trenching war channel her fields,
Nor bruise her flow'rets with the armèd hoofs
Of hostile paces: those opposèd eyes,
10   Which like the meteors of a troubled heaven,
All of one nature, of one substance bred,
Did lately meet in the intestine shock
And furious close of civil butchery,
Shall now, in mutual well-beseeming ranks,
15   March all one way, and be no more opposed
Against acquaintance, kindred, and allies.
The edge of war, like an ill-sheathèd knife,
No more shall cut his master: therefore friends,
As far as to the sepulchre of Christ—
20   Whose soldier now, under whose blessèd cross
We are impressèd and engaged to fight—
Forthwith a power of English shall we levy,
Whose arms were moulded in their mothers' womb
To chase these pagans in those holy fields,
25   Over whose acres walked those blessèd feet
Which fourteen hundred years ago were nailed

---

7. *trenching* i.e., digging military trenches.

10. *meteors* Any unusual disturbances in the sky were assumed in astrology to correspond to troubles on earth. Meteors, all of one heavenly nature, are here compared to the flashing eyes of enemies belonging to the same nationality, in a civil war.

12. *intestine* Of countries, this means "internal."

13. *close* i.e., close combat.

14. *mutual well-beseeming* seeming properly matched to each other.

18. *his* an old genitive form, still sometimes used for "its" in Elizabethan English.

21. *impressèd* conscripted (as in "press-gang"; but the king is "engaged" by a previous vow after the murder of Richard II, rather than forced to go). Here and elsewhere, -èd marks an extra syllable.

22. *power* a normal Elizabethan synonym for an armed force.

23. *mothers'* mothers QqF—the apostrophe could occur before or after the s, depending on whether separate women or a motherland torn by civil war is understood.

For our advantage on the bitter cross.
But this our purpose now is twelve month old,
And bootless 'tis to tell you we will go.
30 Therefore we meet not now: then let me hear
Of you my gentle cousin Westmoreland,
What yesternight our council did decree
In forwarding this dear expedience.

WESTMORELAND

My liege, this haste was hot in question,
35 And many limits of the charge set down
But yesternight, when all athwart there came
A post from Wales, loaden with heavy news,
Whose worst was that the noble Mortimer,
Leading the men of Herefordshire to fight
40 Against the irregular and wild Glendower,
Was by the rude hands of that Welshman taken,
A thousand of his people butcherèd;
Upon whose dead corpse there was such misuse,

---

29. *bootless* useless, literally; without booty, i.e., profit.

30. *therefore* for that, i.e., it is not for that we are meeting now.

31. *cousin* kinsman; Westmoreland married Henry's half-sister.

33. *dear expedience* dear in the sense of much desired; expedience probably meaning the expedition itself, although the main reference is to the speed ("expeditiousness") with which it is intended to execute the plan (see Westmoreland's "this haste" following).

34. *hot in question* debated hotly, or with much questioning of proposals.

35. *limits of the charge set down* leaders' responsibilities (charges) were usually specified (or given limits) in the preparation of the orders for an expedition.

36. *athwart* cutting across (as in the thwarts of boats); interrupting the business.

37. *post* a messenger—from the practice of posting or placing relays along a route to carry messages.

40. *irregular* guerrilla, fighter not in formal military array. *Glendower* two syllables.

43. *corpse* corpes Q1,F; used as in French (*corps,* the reading of Qq2–5) for singular and plural.

Such beastly shameless transformation
45 By those Welshwomen done, as may not be
Without much shame retold, or spoken of.

KING

It seems then that the tidings of this broil
Brake off our business for the Holy Land.

WESTMORELAND

This matched with other did, my gracious lord,
50 For more uneven and unwelcome news
Came from the North, and thus it did import:
On Holy Rood Day the gallant Hotspur there,
Young Harry Percy, and brave Archibald—
That ever valiant and approvèd Scot—
55 At Holmedon met, where they did spend
A sad and bloody hour;
As by discharge of their artillery,
And shape of likelihood the news was told—
For he that brought them, in the very heat
60 And pride of their contention did take horse,
Uncertain of the issue any way.

---

44. *transformation*   a euphemism for mutilation.

50. *uneven*   disrupting. The previous battle in Wales historically occurred nearly three months before this one, on June 22, 1402. Holinshed does not give the date, and Shakespeare heightens the drama by making the battles simultaneous.

52. *Holy Rood Day*   September 14 (1402), the day consecrated to the Holy Cross of Christ.

53. *Archibald*   Earl of Douglas, general of the Scots army.

55. *Holmedon*   in Northumberland; now called Humbleton.

56. The line length is presumably shortened for emphasis—there should be a slight pause after "hour."

57. *artillery*   Despite I.iii.55ff., this did not necessarily mean guns—archers won the battle, in Holinshed.

58. *shape of likelihood*   what appeared probable.

60. *pride*   splendor, highest point (commonly referring to passion).

KING

Here is a dear, a true industrious friend,
Sir Walter Blunt, new lighted from his horse,
Stained with the variation of each soil
65 Betwixt that Holmedon and this seat of ours;
And he hath brought us smooth and welcome news—
The Earl of Douglas is discomfited;
Ten thousand bold Scots, two and twenty knights,
Balked in their own blood, did Sir Walter see
70 On Holmedon's plains; of prisoners Hotspur took
Murdoch, Earl of Fife and eldest son
To beaten Douglas, and the Earl of Athol,
Of Murray, Angus, and Menteith:
And is not this an honorable spoil?
75 A gallant prize—ha, cousin, is it not?

WESTMORELAND

In faith,
It is a conquest for a prince to boast of.

KING

Yea, there thou mak'st me sad, and mak'st me sin

---

62. *is a dear* is deere Qq (corrected in some Q4 texts, Q5,F as given). *true* loyal.

69. *balked* A balk was a ridge in a field, so the dead lay in ridges; but "to balk" also means to frustrate; both meanings are probably intended.

71. *Murdoch* This character is misidentified. He was not, as Holinshed wrote at this point in his history (1807,III,21), "son to the governor Archibald Earl Douglas." A comma after "governor" would have made clear that this was a list of separate prisoners. Murdoch was really son of the regent (or governor) of Scotland, who was the Duke of Albany. On the other hand, the Earl of Athol, etc., is not historically another person as he appears in the following lines, for all the titles belonged to Murdoch. Again, the mistake is Holinshed's.

75–6. Q reads "*King:* . . . is it not? In faith it is./*West.:* A conquest. . . ." The lineation adopted here was suggested by Steevens. Westmoreland was almost certainly intended to have the short line, as the big gap in Q1 suggests.

In envy, that my Lord Northumberland
80 Should be the father to so blest a son:
A son, who is the theme of honour's tongue,
Amongst a grove the very straightest plant,
Who is sweet Fortune's minion and her pride;
Whilst I by looking on the praise of him
85 See riot and dishonor stain the brow
Of my young Harry. O that it could be proved
That some night-tripping fairy had exchanged
In cradle-clothes our children where they lay,
And called mine Percy, his Plantagenet!
90 Then would I have his Harry, and he mine;
But let him from my thoughts. What think you, coz,
Of this young Percy's pride? The prisoners
Which he in this adventure hath surprised
To his own use he keeps, and sends me word
95 I shall have none but Murdoch, Earl of Fife.

WESTMORELAND

This is his uncle's teaching, this is Worcester,
Malevolent to you in all aspects—

---

83. *minion*   darling (French, *mignonne*).

87. *fairy*   Folk lore abounds in tales of such mischievous exchanges of bad children ("changelings") for good ones by fairies. The remark implies that Hotspur and the Prince were roughly the same age, as the poet Daniel makes them in his *Civil Wars*, though historically Hotspur was by twenty-three years the elder.

89. *Plantagenet*   family name of the French dynasty from which the English royal family was descended.

95. *none but Murdoch*   The rules of war required that, as a member of the Scots royal family, he be handed over to the King. A. R. Humphreys quotes Sir J. Turner, *Pallas Armata* (1683), p. 341: "The ransom of a prisoner belongs to him who took him, unless he be a person of very eminent quality." See also the passage in Holinshed (Appendix B, p. 158).

96. *Worcester*   two syllables ("wŏŏs'ter").

97. *malevolent . . . aspects*   These terms, taken from astrology, imply that Worcester exercises a hostile influence over the fortunes of Henry comparable to that of an unfavorable planet.

Which makes him prune himself, and bristle up
The crest of youth against your dignity.

KING

100   But I have sent for him to answer this;
And for this cause awhile we must neglect
Our holy purpose to Jerusalem.
Cousin, on Wednesday next our council we
Will hold at Windsor, so inform the lords—
105   But come yourself with speed to us again;
For more is to be said and to be done
Than out of anger can be utterèd.

WESTMORELAND

I will, my liege.

Exeunt.

[*Scene ii: Elsewhere in London.*] *Enter* PRINCE OF WALES *and*
SIR JOHN FALSTAFF.

FALSTAFF

Now Hal, what time of day is it, lad?

PRINCE

Thou art so fat-witted with drinking of old sack, and unbutton-
ing thee after supper, and sleeping upon benches after noon,
that thou hast forgotten to demand that truly which thou
5   wouldst truly know. What a Devil hast thou to do with the time
of the day? Unless hours were cups of sack, and minutes capons, and clocks the tongues of bawds, and dials the signs of

---

98. *prune*   preen, a gesture characteristic of birds of prey prepar-
ing for action.
107. *out of anger*   in a state of anger. *utterèd*   made public.
2. *sack*   a class of white wines, like sherry, often dry in flavor
(compare French *sec*), imported from Spain in Shakespeare's time.
5. *a Devil*   in the Devil['s name] (see p. 168).
6–7. *capons*   fowls for eating. *dials*   clock faces.

leaping-houses, and the blessed Sun himself a fair hot wench
in flame-coloured taffeta, I see no reason why thou shouldst be
10   so superfluous to demand the time of the day.

FALSTAFF

Indeed, you come near me now, Hal, for we that take purses go
by the moon and the seven stars, and not "by Phoebus, he, that
wand'ring knight so fair." And I prithee, sweet wag, when
thou art a king, as God save thy grace (majesty, I should say,
15   for grace thou wilt have none) . . .

PRINCE

What none?

FALSTAFF

No, by my troth, not so much as will serve to be prologue to an
egg and butter.

PRINCE

Well, how then? Come, roundly, roundly!

FALSTAFF

20   Marry then, sweet wag, when thou art king let not us that are
Squires of the Night's Body, be called "thieves of the day's

---

8. *leaping-houses*   brothels.

9. *taffeta*   In *AW*, II.ii.22 Shakespeare mentions a prostitute
dressed in taffeta.

12. *seven stars*   the Pleiades.

12–13. *"by Phoebus . . . fair"*   This archaic use of "he" (see p. 168)
is noted by the *OED* as characteristic of ballads. Phoebus is the Greek
sun god; but the Knight of the Sun is the hero of a popular Spanish
romance, called in translation *The Mirror of Princely Deeds and
Knighthood* (1578), from which the ballad may derive.

13. *wag*   witty person.

14–15. *grace . . .*   a triple pun, as grace may be a salutation like
"majesty," grace in the theological sense, or grace before a meal, not
to mention physical grace.

19. *roundly*   smartly (but with a pun on Falstaff's girth).

20ff. *Marry then . . .*   Falstaff's punning speech ("body" may be
pronounced "bawdy") amounts to saying that he rejects criticism of
his idleness by day because he works by night.

beauty": let us be "Diana's Foresters"—gentlemen of the
shade, minions of the Moon; and let men say we be men of
good government, being governed as the sea is, by our noble
25   and chaste mistress the Moon, under whose countenance we
steal.

PRINCE

Thou sayest well, and it holds well too, for the fortune of us
that are the Moon's men doth ebb and flow like the sea, being
governed as the sea is by the Moon. As for proof now, a purse
30   of gold most resolutely snatched on Monday night and most
dissolutely spent on Tuesday morning, got with swearing "Lay
by!" and spent with crying "Bring in!"; now in as low an ebb
as the foot of the ladder; and by and by in as high a flow as the
ridge of the gallows.

FALSTAFF

35   By the Lord thou say say'st true, lad; and is not my hostess of
the tavern a most sweet wench?

PRINCE

As the honey of Hybla, my old lad of the castle—and is not a
buff jerkin a most sweet robe of durance?

---

22. *"Diana's Foresters"*   a mock title (like "Squires of the Night's
Body") alluding to Diana's role as goddess of hunting as well as of the
moon; she thus, like thieves, was associated with forests.

25. *countenance*   face, but also patronage.

31–2. *"Lay by!"*   "put down your money (or weapons)"—a highwayman's challenge. *"Bring in!"*   order to a waiter.

33. *ladder*   leading to the ridge or top of the gallows from which
the criminal fell to execution.

35–6. *my hostess . . . wench*   The hostess in Eastcheap, at least, is
no longer attractive. This, like Hal's answer, may be a now ironic detail from an earlier version of the play (see p. 165). Falstaff is trying to
change the subject to pleasanter topics than gallows, at least.

37. *Hybla*   Sicilian town famous for its honey. *my old lad of the
castle*   an allusion to Falstaff's original name in the play; but taverns
were called the "devil's castle" in medieval sermons (see Owst's *Literature and the Pulpit*, Cambridge, England, 1933, p. 438).

38. *buff jerkin*   a leather jacket worn by constables; hence the play
on "durance," which means both "hard-wearing" and "imprisonment."

FALSTAFF

How now, how now, mad wag? What, in thy quips and thy
40   quiddities? What a plague have I to do with a buff jerkin?

PRINCE

Why, what a pox have I to do with my hostess of the tavern?

FALSTAFF

Well, thou hast called her to a reckoning many a time and oft.

PRINCE

Did I ever call for thee to pay thy part?

FALSTAFF

No, I'll give thee thy due, thou hast paid all there.

PRINCE

45   Yea, and elsewhere, so far as my coin would stretch; and where
it would not, I have used my credit.

FALSTAFF

Yea, and so used it that were it not here apparent that thou art
heir apparent . . . But I prithee sweet wag, shall there be gallows standing in England when thou art king?—and resolution
50   thus fobbed as it is with the rusty curb of old father Antic, the
law? Do not thou, when thou art king, hang a thief.

PRINCE

No, thou shalt.

FALSTAFF

Shall I? O rare! By the Lord, I'll be a brave judge.

PRINCE

Thou judgest false already—I mean thou shalt have the hang-
55   ing of the thieves, and so become a rare hangman.

---

40. *quiddities* quibbles—from *quidditas,* "whatness," a word used
in medieval Latin disputations.
48. *heir apparent . . .* "you would get no more credit" is understood.
50. *fobbed* cheated. *Antic* an "antic" was a buffoon or clown.
53. *brave* fine.

FALSTAFF

Well, Hal, well—and in some sort it jumps with my humour—
as well as waiting in the court, I can tell you.

PRINCE

For obtaining of suits?

FALSTAFF

Yea, for obtaining of suits, whereof the hangman hath no lean
60   wardrobe. 'Sblood, I am as melancholy as a gib cat, or a lugged
bear.

PRINCE

Or an old lion, or a lover's lute.

FALSTAFF

Yea, or the drone of a Lincolnshire bagpipe.

PRINCE

What sayest thou to a hare, or the melancholy of Moor-Ditch?

FALSTAFF

65   Thou hast the most unsavoury similes, and art indeed the most
comparative, rascalliest—sweet, young prince. But Hal, I

---

56. *jumps with my humour* matches my temperament. "Jump"
was also slang for "hang."

59. *suits* At court, a suit was a solicitation for employment; the
hangman was given the clothing, or suits, of his victims.

60. *gib cat* (castrated?) tom cat; cats are often held to have gloomy
associations (as in Poe's "The Tell-Tale Heart"). *lugged* baited; or,
simply, dragged captive.

63. *Lincolnshire bagpipe* Like the Scots bagpipe, often held to be
dreary, particularly the "drone" or bass note.

64. *hare* as a timorous, hunted animal traditionally a symbol of
melancholy. *Moor-Ditch* Steevens quotes Stow's *Survey* about this
open sewer, draining Moorfield Marshes near Bedlam Hospital and
skirting north London: "a very narrow, and the same a filthy channel";
and Malone cites J. Taylor's *Pennyless Pilgrimage* (1618), "my mind
attired with moody, muddy Moore-ditch melancholy."

65. *similes* Q5. Qq1–4,F read *smiles*.

66. *comparative* cf. *LLL*, V.ii.852, "Full of comparisons and
wounding flouts."

prithee trouble me no more with vanity. I would to God thou and I knew where a commodity of good names were to be bought. An old lord of the Council rated me the other day in
70 the street about you, sir, but I marked him not; and yet he talked very wisely, but I regarded him not; and yet he talked wisely and in the street too.

PRINCE

Thou didst well, for wisdom cries out in the streets and no man regards it.

FALSTAFF

75 O, thou hast damnable iteration, and art indeed able to corrupt a saint: thou hast done much harm upon me Hal, God forgive thee for it! Before I knew thee, Hal, I knew nothing, and now am I, if a man should speak truly, little better than one of the wicked. I must give over this life, and I will give it over. By the
80 Lord, and I do not, I am a villain! I'll be damned for never a king's son in Christendom.

PRINCE

Where shall we take a purse tomorrow, Jack?

FALSTAFF

'Zounds, where thou wilt, lad; I'll make one—an I do not, call me "villain" and baffle me.

---

68. *commodity* supply.

69. *Council* presumably the Privy Council, the King's close advisers.

73–4. *wisdom cries* . . . "Wisdom crieth without . . . in the streets"; "I have stretched out mine hand, and none would regard. But ye have despised all my counsel." Proverbs 1:20*ff.*

75. *damnable iteration* The Devil is supposed to quote freely from ("iterate") Scripture; this whole passage, like much of Falstaff, parodies Puritan cant. Oldcastle, the historical model for Falstaff, was a follower of Wycliff, forerunner of the Reformation.

80. *and* Like "an," "and" could mean "if" in Elizabethan English; see Appendix C, p. 170.

83. *'Zounds* "By God's wounds", an oath sufficiently strong for F to censor it.

84. *baffle* to degrade a knight by turning his arms, or picture, or

PRINCE

85 I see a good amendment of life in thee, from praying to purse-
taking.

FALSTAFF

Why Hal, 'tis my vocation, Hal; 'tis no sin for a man to labour
in his vocation.

Enter POINS.

Poins! Now shall we know if Gadshill have set a match. O, if
90 men were to be saved by merit, what hole in hell were hot
enough for him? This is the most omnipotent villain that ever
cried "Stand!" to a true man.

PRINCE

Good morrow, Ned.

POINS

Good morrow, sweet Hal. What says Monsieur Remorse?
95 What says Sir John Sack and Sugar? Jack, how agrees the Devil
and thee about thy soul, that thou soldest him on Good Friday
last for a cup of Madeira and a cold capon's leg?

PRINCE

Sir John stands to his word; the Devil shall have his bargain,

---

even his body upside down—compare Spenser's *Faerie Queene*, VI.vii.
27: "He by the heels him hung upon a tree,/ And baffled so that all
which passèd by,/ The picture of his punishment might see."
  87. *vocation* . . . a popular puritan text was I Corinthians 7:20:
"Let every man abide in the same vocation wherein he was called."
  89. *Gadshill* The nickname a thief in *The Famous Victories* acquired from the locale of his crimes is here made a proper name. The
hill, near Rochester on the road from London to Kent, was a spot favored by highwaymen because it slowed travelers down. *set a match*
arranged a game (i.e., a robbery).
  90. *saved by merit* Falstaff naturally follows the Puritans who
claimed virtue was no guarantee of salvation without God's grace, but
he asserts that if they were wrong as Catholics claim, and good works
counted, then Poins must be damned.
  95. *Sack and Sugar? Jack* Sacke, and Sugar Iacke? Qq. Falstaff's
dry wine needs sweetening to suit his taste.
  96. *Good Friday* The strictest fast day; hence, a day of great
temptation to sin for Falstaff.

for he was never yet a breaker of proverbs: he will "give the
100   Devil his due."

POINS

Then art thou damned for keeping thy word with the Devil.

PRINCE

Else he had been damned for cozening the Devil.

POINS

But my lads, my lads, tomorrow morning, by four o'clock early
at Gad's Hill, there are pilgrims going to Canterbury with rich
105   offerings, and traders riding to London with fat purses. I have
vizards for you all, you have horses for yourselves; Gadshill
lies tonight in Rochester; I have bespoke supper tomorrow
night in Eastcheap: we may do it as secure as sleep. If you will
go, I will stuff your purses full of crowns: if you will not, tarry
110   at home and be hanged.

FALSTAFF

Hear ye, Yedward, if I tarry at home and go not, I'll hang you
for going.

POINS

You will, chops?

FALSTAFF

Hal, wilt thou make one?

PRINCE

115   Who, I rob? I a thief? Not I, by my faith.

FALSTAFF

There's neither honesty, manhood, nor good fellowship in thee,
nor thou cam'st not of the blood royal, if thou darest not stand
for ten shillings.

---

102. *cozening*   deceiving.
106. *vizards*   visors or masks.
108. *Eastcheap*   the location of the Boar's Head Tavern, haunt of
Falstaff and his friends. Eastcheap means "east market."
111. *Yedward*   dialect form of Edward.
113. *chops*   jaws.
117. *royal*   a pun; a royal was worth ten shillings. *stand for*   be
worth; also, challenge someone for.

HAL

Well then, once in my days I'll be a madcap.

FALSTAFF

120 Why that's well said.

PRINCE

Well, come what will, I'll tarry at home.

FALSTAFF

By the Lord, I'll be a traitor then, when thou art king.

PRINCE

I care not.

POINS

Sir John, I prithee leave the prince and me alone; I will lay
125 him down such reasons for this adventure that he shall go.

FALSTAFF

Well, God give thee the spirit of persuasion, and him the ears
of profiting, that what thou speakest may move, and what he
hears may be believed, that the true prince may (for recreation sake) prove a false thief, for the poor abuses of the time
130 want countenance. Farewell; you shall find me in Eastcheap.

PRINCE

Farewell, the latter spring! Farewell, All-hallown summer!

[*Exit* FALSTAFF.]

POINS

Now, my good sweet honey lord, ride with us tomorrow. I have
a jest to execute that I cannot manage alone. Falstaff, Bardolph,
Peto, and Gadshill shall rob those men that we have already

---

130. *countenance* public approval. In this sentence Falstaff again
parodies puritan sententiousness, while admonishing his hearers to evil
courses.

131. *the* thou, vocative of the definite article. *All-hallown summer*
"Indian summer", as All Hallows is All Saints Day, November 1. The
prince means that Falstaff's faculties have fitfully survived their maturity.

133–4. *Bardolph, Peto* Haruey, Rossill Qq; probably names belonging to the original version, like that of Oldcastle, but here acci-

135   waylaid; yourself and I will not be there: and when they have
the booty, if you and I do not rob them, cut this head off from
my shoulders.

PRINCE

How shall we part with them in setting forth?

POINS

Why, we will set forth before or after them, and appoint them
140   a place of meeting, wherein it is at our pleasure to fail; and
then will they adventure upon the exploit themselves, which
they shall have no sooner achieved but we'll set upon them.

PRINCE

Yea, but 'tis like that they will know us by our horses, by our
habits, and by every other appointment to be ourselves.

POINS

145   Tut, our horses they shall not see, I'll tie them in the wood;
our vizards we will change after we leave them; and, sirrah, I
have cases of buckram for the nonce, to immask our noted out-
ward garments.

PRINCE

Yea, but I doubt they will be too hard for us.

POINS

150   Well, for two of them, I know them to be as true-bred cowards
as ever turned back; and for the third, if he fight longer than
he sees reason, I'll forswear arms. The virtue of this jest will
be the incomprehensible lies that this same fat rogue will tell
us when we meet at supper—how thirty at least he fought with,

---

dentally left unchanged. Otherwise, possibly actors' names. The
quartos give the speech prefix *"Ross"* (= Rossill?) to three speeches
by Gadshill (II.iv.151,153,157).

144. *appointment*   equipment.

146. *sirrah*   a familiar form of "sir" (compare I.iii.117), here used
indecorously by Poins to the Prince.

147. *cases of buckram for the nonce*   suits of coarse cloth for the
purpose.

149. *doubt*   fear.

155   what wards, what blows, what extremities he endured; and in
       the reproof of this lives the jest.

                              PRINCE

       Well, I'll go with thee—provide us all things necessary; and
       meet me tomorrow night in Eastcheap, there I'll sup. Farewell.

                              POINS

       Farewell, my lord.

                                                    Exit [POINS.]

                              PRINCE

160   I know you all, and will awhile uphold
       The unyoked humour of your idleness;
       Yet herein will I imitate the sun,
       Who doth permit the base contagious clouds
       To smother up his beauty from the world,
165   That when he please again to be himself,
       Being wanted he may be more wondered at
       By breaking through the foul and ugly mists
       Of vapours that did seem to strangle him.
       If all the year were playing holidays,
170   To sport would be as tedious as to work;
       But when they seldom come, they wished for come;
       And nothing pleaseth but rare accidents:
       So when this loose behaviour I throw off,
       And pay the debt I never promisèd,
175   By how much better than my word I am,
       By so much shall I falsify men's hopes;
       And like bright metal on a sullen ground,
       My reformation glitt'ring o'er my fault

---

       155. *wards*   parries.
       158. *tomorrow night*   Hal is thinking of their confrontation of Fal-
       staff the next evening, not of their going to the robbery (during the
       present night).
       161. *unyoked humour*   unrestrained temper.
       163. *contagious*   pestilential (clouds were thought to carry disease,
       see also *RII*, III.iii.86–7).
       177. *sullen ground*   dark background.

Shall show more goodly, and attract more eyes
180   Than that which hath no foil to set it off.
I'll so offend, to make offence a skill,
Redeeming time when men think least I will.

Exit.

[*Scene iii: Windsor Castle.*] *Enter the* KING, NORTHUMBERLAND,
WORCESTER, HOTSPUR, SIR WALTER BLUNT, *with others.*

KING

My blood hath been too cold and temperate,
Unapt to stir at these indignities,
And you have found me, for accordingly
You tread upon my patience; but be sure
5   I will from henceforth rather be myself
Mighty and to be feared, than my condition
Which hath been smooth as oil, soft as young down,
And therefore lost that title of respect,
Which the proud soul ne'er pays but to the proud.

WORCESTER

10   Our house, my sovereign liege, little deserves
The scourge of greatness to be used on it,
And that same greatness too, which our own hands
Have holp to make so portly.

NORTHUMBERLAND

My lord . . .

---

182. *redeeming time* atoning for wasted time. *will* Here, as
often, the rhyming couplet signals the end of the scene and provides
a cue for the start of a new scene.
S.D. *Windsor Castle* see I.i.104.
3. *found me* found me out.
13. *holp* archaic form for "helped"; the Percys were Henry's principal supporters in defying and overthrowing Richard II. *portly* ma-
jestic.

KING

Worcester get thee gone, for I do see
15 Danger, and disobedience in thine eye:
O sir, your presence is too bold and peremptory,
And Majesty might never yet endure
The moody frontier of a servant brow.
You have good leave to leave us—when we need
20 Your use and counsel we shall send for you.

Exit WORCESTER.

You were about to speak.

NORTHUMBERLAND

Yea, my good lord.
Those prisoners in your highness' name demanded,
Which Harry Percy here at Holmedon took,
Were, as he says, not with such strength denied
25 As is delivered to your majesty.
Either envy therefore, or misprision,
Is guilty of this fault, and not my son.

HOTSPUR

My liege, I did deny no prisoners,
But I remember, when the fight was done,
30 When I was dry with rage, and extreme toil,
Breathless and faint, leaning upon my sword,
Came there a certain lord, neat and trimly dressed,
Fresh as a bridegroom, and his chin new reaped
Showed like a stubble-land at harvest-home;
35 He was perfumèd like a milliner,
And 'twixt his finger and his thumb he held

---

18. *moody frontier of a servant brow*   a play on "front" (French:
forehead) and frontier in the sense of an armed boundary—kings re-
sent an angry subject's frowns.
26. *misprision*   mistake.
27. *is guilty of*   is to be blamed (for inventing).
33. *reaped*   with a fashionable short beard, rather than clean-
shaven.

A pouncet-box, which ever and anon
He gave his nose and took't away again—
Who therewith angry, when it next came there
40 Took it in snuff; and still he smiled and talked;
And as the soldiers bore dead bodies by,
He called them untaught knaves, unmannerly,
To bring a slovenly unhandsome corpse
Betwixt the wind and his nobility.
45 With many holiday and lady terms
He questioned me—amongst the rest demanded
My prisoners in your majesty's behalf.
I then all smarting, with my wounds being cold,
To be so pestered with a popinjay,
50 Out of my grief and my impatience
Answered neglectingly I know not what—
He should, or he should not—for he made me mad
To see him shine so brisk, and smell so sweet,
And talk so like a waiting-gentlewoman
55 Of guns, and drums, and wounds, God save the mark!
And telling me the sovereignest thing on earth

---

37. *pouncet box*   Pounce (derived from Latin *pumex*: pumice) was powder used to dry ink; the small sprinkling box used could be filled with perfumed materials (e.g., orange peel) to smother unpleasant odors.

40. *took it in snuff*   The courtier's nose reacted to the bad odor when the perfume was removed and sniffed the perfume again with a snort like an angry person's. Tobacco snuff appears only after 1600.

45. *holiday and lady terms*   trivial and effeminate expressions.

49. *popinjay*   a brilliantly colored bird, like a parrot.

50. *grief*   pain (see V.i.131).

54. *waiting-gentlewoman*   a court lady employed in the personal service of royalty.

55. *mark*   the cross—the phrase calls a blessing on the cross and is comparable to crossing oneself, as Hotspur might half ironically do here in mentioning wounds and similar misfortunes (compare *Oth*, I.i.33: "*Iago*: And I—God bless the mark—his Moorship's ancient").

56. *sovereignest*   most powerful (literally: most kingly).

Was parmaceti, for an inward bruise,
And that it was great pity, so it was,
This villainous saltpetre should be digged
60   Out of the bowels of the harmless earth,
Which many a good tall fellow had destroyed
So cowardly, and but for these vile guns
He would himself have been a soldier.
This bald, unjointed chat of his, my lord,
65   I answered indirectly, as I said,
And I beseech you, let not his report
Come current for an accusation
Betwixt my love and your high majesty.

BLUNT

The circumstances considered, good my lord,
70   What e'er Lord Harry Percy then had said
To such a person, and in such a place,
At such a time, with all the rest retold,
May reasonably die, and never rise
To do him wrong, or anyway impeach
75   What then he said, so he unsay it now.

KING

Why, yet he doth deny his prisoners,
But with proviso and exception—
That we at our own charge shall ransom straight
His brother-in-law, the foolish Mortimer,
80   Who, on my soul, hath wilfully betrayed
The lives of those that he did lead to fight
Against that great magician, damned Glendower,

---

57. *parmaceti* spermaceti, an oil from the head of sperm whales, still used for cosmetics. The text's misspelling comes from a false etymology supposing the "medicinal" ointment came from Parma in Italy.
61. *tall* brave (still used, though archaic).
64. *bald* flat.
79. *brother-in-law* Hotspur married Mortimer's sister, Elizabeth (called Kate in this play).

Whose daughter, as we hear, that Earl of March
Hath lately married: shall our coffers then
85   Be emptied to redeem a traitor home?
Shall we buy treason? and indent with fears
When they have lost and forfeited themselves?
No, on the barren mountains let him starve!
For I shall never hold that man my friend
90   Whose tongue shall ask me for one penny cost
To ransom home revolted Mortimer.

                    HOTSPUR

Revolted Mortimer! . . .
He never did fall off, my sovereign liege,
But by the chance of war. To prove that true
95   Needs no more but one tongue for all those wounds,
Those mouthèd wounds which valiantly he took,
When on the gentle Severn's sedgy bank,
In single opposition hand-to-hand,
He did confound the best part of an hour
100 In changing hardiment with great Glendower;
Three times they breathed and three times did they drink
Upon agreement of swift Severn's flood,
Who then affrighted with their bloody looks,
Ran fearfully among the trembling reeds,
105 And hid his crisp head in the hollow bank,
Bloodstained with these valiant combatants.

---

83. *Earl* . . .   The Edmund Mortimer (1376–1409) who fought Glendower and married his daughter was actually not the Earl of March
(Roger Mortimer), but the younger brother of this earl, whose son and
successor to the title happens also to have been called Edmund Mortimer (1391–1425)—hence the confusion (see genealogy, p. xxviii).
86. *indent*   contract. *fears*   fears of traitors.
99. *confound*   utterly use up.
100. *changing hardiment*   exchanging brave acts, or bravery.
105. *crisp*   rippling; but with a play on the use of "head," which
here means both surface, and pressure of current (compare "head of
steam").

Never did bare and rotten policy
Colour her working with such deadly wounds,
Nor never could the noble Mortimer
110 Receive so many, and all willingly:
Then let not him be slandered with revolt.

KING

Thou dost belie him, Percy, thou dost belie him—
He never did encounter with Glendower:
I tell thee—
115 He durst as well have met the Devil alone
As Owen Glendower for an enemy.
Art thou not ashamed? . . . But sirrah, henceforth
Let me not hear you speak of Mortimer:
Send me your prisoners with the speediest means,
120 Or you shall hear in such a kind from me
As will displease you. My Lord Northumberland:
We license your departure with your son;
Send us your prisoners, or you will hear of it.

Exit KING [*with all his followers*].

HOTSPUR

And if the Devil come and roar for them
125 I will not send them: I will after straight
And tell him so, for I will ease my heart,
Albeit I make a hazard of my head.

NORTHUMBERLAND

What, drunk with choler? Stay, and pause awhile,
Here comes your uncle.

Enter WORCESTER.

---

107. *bare* open (barefaced) or wretched (threadbare?).
114. This short line and the next appear as one in Qq,F; the present form makes clear the irregularity and emphasis of the King's speech. Many lines in this scene are irregular, to mark dramatic emphasis. See the relevant passage from Holinshed, Appendix B, p. 159.
120. *kind* manner.
128. *choler* a bodily fluid supposed to foster anger.

HOTSPUR

Speak of Mortimer?

130 'Zounds, I will speak of him, and let my soul
Want mercy if I do not join with him:
Yea, on his part I'll empty all these veins,
And shed my dear blood, drop by drop in the dust,
But I will lift the down-trod Mortimer

135 As high in the air as this unthankful king,
As this ingrate and cankered Bolingbroke.

NORTHUMBERLAND

Brother, the king hath made your nephew mad.

WORCESTER

Who struck this heat up after I was gone?

HOTSPUR

He will forsooth have all my prisoners,

140 And when I urged the ransom once again
Of my wife's brother, then his cheek looked pale,
And on my face he turned an eye of death,
Trembling even at the name of Mortimer.

WORCESTER

I cannot blame him: was not he proclaimed

145 By Richard that dead is, the next of blood?

NORTHUMBERLAND

He was, I heard the proclamation;
And then it was, when the unhappy king
(Whose wrongs in us God pardon!) did set forth

---

136. *cankered* corrupt. *Bolingbroke* Before his accession the King was often known as Henry of Bolingbroke, because he was born at Bolingbroke Castle in Lincolnshire. Hotspur treats Henry like a commoner by using this name rather than his titles.

139. *forsooth* truly.

144. *proclaimed* Edmund Mortimer is again mistaken for his brother Roger Mortimer, who was proclaimed heir, because the latter's son, also called Edmund, did inherit this claim against King Henry's throne. Shakespeare combines the attributes of the two Edmunds here.

148. *Whose wrongs in us* our wrongs against whom.

Upon his Irish expedition;
150 From whence he, intercepted, did return
To be deposed, and shortly murderèd.

WORCESTER

And for whose death we in the world's wide mouth
Live scandalized and foully spoken of.

HOTSPUR

But soft, I pray you, did King Richard then
155 Proclaim my brother Edmund Mortimer
Heir to the crown?

NORTHUMBERLAND
He did, myself did hear it.

HOTSPUR

Nay, then I cannot blame his cousin king,
That wished him on the barren mountains starve.
But shall it be that you that set the crown
160 Upon the head of this forgetful man,
And for his sake wear the detested blot
Of murderous subornation—shall it be
That you a world of curses undergo,
Being the agents, or base second means,
165 The cords, the ladder, or the hangman rather—
O pardon me, that I descend so low
To show the line and the predicament
Wherein you range under this subtle king!—
Shall it for shame be spoken in these days,
170 Or fill up chronicles in time to come,
That men of your nobility and power

---

150. *intercepted*   interrupted.
153. *scandalized*   made the subject of scandal.
154. *soft*   wait a moment.
162. *murderous subornation*   being accessories to murder.
164. *second means*   not primary; hence, mere agents of another.
167. *line and the predicament*   level and nature. "Predicament" in logic meant "category," but both it and "line" also recall "hangman" earlier.

Did gage them both in an unjust behalf
(As both of you, God pardon it, have done)
To put down Richard, that sweet lovely rose,
175 And plant this thorn, this canker Bolingbroke?
And shall it in more shame be further spoken,
That you are fooled, discarded, and shook off
By him for whom these shames ye underwent?
No!—yet time serves, wherein you may redeem
180 Your banished honours, and restore yourselves
Into the good thoughts of the world again:
Revenge the jeering and disdained contempt
Of this proud king, who studies day and night
To answer all the debt he owes to you,
185 Even with the bloody payment of your deaths:
Therefore, I say . . .

WORCESTER

         Peace, cousin, say no more;
And now I will unclasp a secret book,
And to your quick-conceiving discontents
I'll read you matter deep and dangerous,
190 As full of peril and adventurous spirit,
As to o'erwalk a current roaring loud
On the unsteadfast footing of a spear.

HOTSPUR

If he fall in, good night, or sink or swim!
Send danger from the east unto the west,
195 So honour cross it from the north to south,

---

172. *gage*   pledge.

175. *canker*   wild or "dog" rose; also: ulcer; caterpillar; and a rot in fruit trees—all applicable metaphorically here.

182. *disdained*   endowed with disdain.

191–2. *o'erwalk . . . spear*   Humphreys notes that this is a popular motif in such romances as Chrétien de Troyes' *Erec and Enid* (see Everyman edn., p. 308).

193. *good night, or sink or swim*   we must bid him adieu, as bound to drown, whether he struggles or sinks at once.

195. *so*   provided.

And let them grapple. O the blood more stirs
To rouse a lion than to start a hare!

NORTHUMBERLAND

Imagination of some great exploit
Drives him beyond the bounds of patience.

[HOTSPUR]

200 By heaven, methinks it were an easy leap
To pluck bright honour from the pale-faced moon,
Or dive into the bottom of the deep,
Where fathom-line could never touch the ground,
And pluck up drownèd Honour by the locks,
205 So he that doth redeem her thence might wear
Without corrival all her dignities—
But out upon this half-faced fellowship!

WORCESTER

He apprehends a world of figures here,
But not the form of what he should attend.
210 Good cousin, give me audience for a while.

HOTSPUR

I cry you mercy.

WORCESTER

Those same noble Scots
That are your prisoners, . . .

HOTSPUR

I'll keep them all;
By God he shall not have a Scot of them,

200–207. These lines are given to Northumberland by Qq1–4, but
the style and context make it clear that the later attributions to
Hotspur are correct, as in Q5,F.

206. *corrival* competitor.

207. *half-faced fellowship* the comradely sharing of honors, which
are thinned to a mere profile like a coin's.

208. *apprehends* conceives. *figures* figures of speech, or fancies.

213. *Scot* a pun, since Scot might mean Scotsman, but was also a
minor tax payment.

No, if a Scot would save his soul he shall not:
215   I'll keep them, by this hand!

WORCESTER

                     You start away,
And lend no ear unto my purposes:
Those prisoners you shall keep . . .

HOTSPUR

                          Nay I will: that's flat!
He said he would not ransom Mortimer,
Forbade my tongue to speak of Mortimer;
220   But I will find him when he lies asleep,
And in his ear I'll hollo "Mortimer!"
Nay—I'll have a starling shall be taught to speak
Nothing but "Mortimer," and give it him
To keep his anger still in motion.

WORCESTER

225   Hear you, cousin, a word . . .

HOTSPUR

All studies here I solemnly defy,
Save how to gall and pinch this Bolingbroke;
And that same sword-and-buckler Prince of Wales,
But that I think his father loves him not,
230   And would be glad he met with some mischance,
I would have him poisoned with a pot of ale.

WORCESTER

Farewell, kinsman—I'll talk to you
When you are better tempered to attend.

NORTHUMBERLAND

Why, what a wasp-stung and impatient fool
235   Art thou, to break into this woman's mood,

---

226. *defy*   repudiate.
228. *sword-and-buckler*   In comparison with the gentleman's rapier, these were servants' arms by Shakespeare's time.
231. *ale*   Hotspur means that Hal does not drink wine like a gentleman.

Tying thine ear to no tongue but thine own!

HOTSPUR

Why, look you, I am whipped and scourged with rods,
Nettled, and stung with pismires, when I hear
Of this vile politician Bolingbroke.
240   In Richard's time—what do you call the place?
A plague upon it, it is in Gloucestershire;
'Twas where the mad-cap Duke his uncle kept,
His uncle York—where I first bowed my knee
Unto this king of smiles, this Bolingbroke—
245   'Sblood!—when you and he came back from Ravenspurgh.

NORTHUMBERLAND

At Berkeley Castle.

HOTSPUR

You say true.
Why what a candy deal of courtesy
This fawning greyhound then did proffer me:
"Look when his infant fortune came to age . . . ,"
250   And "gentle Harry Percy," and "kind cousin"—
O, the Devil take such cozeners!—God forgive me!
Good uncle, tell your tale—I have done.

WORCESTER

Nay, if you have not, to it again—
We will stay your leisure.

HOTSPUR
I have done i'faith.

---

238. *pismires* ants.

242. *kept* resided.

245. *Ravenspurgh* a Yorkshire port, since washed away by the
sea, where Henry first landed on returning from exile in 1399.

247. *candy deal* sweet (i.e., flattering) amount; the quoted phrases
appear in *RII*, II.iii.

249. *Look when* whenever (a dialect expression); compare *RIII*,
I.iii.290, "Look when he fawns, he bites."

251. *cozeners* cheats; also, a pun on Henry's use of "kind cousin,"
which provides an etymology for the word.

WORCESTER

255   Then once more to your Scottish prisoners:
        Deliver them up without their ransom straight,
        And make the Douglas' son your only mean
        For powers in Scotland, which, for diverse reasons
        Which I shall send you written, be assured
260   Will easily be granted. You, my lord, [*to* NORTH.]
        Your son in Scotland being thus employed,
        Shall secretly into the bosom creep
        Of that same noble prelate well beloved,
        The Archbishop . . .

HOTSPUR
Of York, is it not?

WORCESTER

265   True . . . who bears hard
        His brother's death at Bristol—the Lord Scroop.
        I speak not this in estimation,
        As what I think might be, but what I know
        Is ruminated, plotted, and set down,
270   And only stays but to behold the face
        Of that occasion that shall bring it on.

HOTSPUR
I smell it. Upon my life, it will do well!

NORTHUMBERLAND
Before the game is afoot thou still let'st slip.

---

257. *the Douglas'*   The head of a Scots family was called by its
name, preceded by "the."
    266. *Bristol*   Qq have "Bristow"; William Scrope, Earl of Wilt-
shire, was executed there as a traitor in 1399, but he was actually the
Archbishop's cousin. The mistake is Holinshed's.
    267. *estimation*   guesswork.
    273. *still*   always. *slip*   unleash [the hunting dogs]. "You always
let the hounds loose before the quarry starts to run"; i.e., you always
talk before the issues are clear. Northumberland continues the hunting
image suggested by Hotspur's "I smell it."

HOTSPUR

Why, it cannot choose but be a noble plot!
275 And then the power of Scotland, and of York,
To join with Mortimer, ha?

WORCESTER

        And so they shall.

HOTSPUR

In faith, it is exceedingly well aimed.

WORCESTER

And 'tis no little reason bids us speed,
To save our heads by raising of a head—
280 For, bear ourselves as even as we can,
The king will always think him in our debt,
And think we think ourselves unsatisfied,
Till he hath found a time to pay us home.
And see already how he doth begin
285 To make us strangers to his looks of love.

HOTSPUR

He does, he does! We'll be revenged on him.

WORCESTER

Cousin, farewell. No further go in this
Than I by letters shall direct your course.
When time is ripe, which will be suddenly,
290 I'll steal to Glendower and Lord Mortimer,
Where you and Douglas, and our powers at once,
As I will fashion it, shall happily meet,
To bear our fortunes in our own strong arms,
Which now we hold at much uncertainty.

NORTHUMBERLAND

295 Farewell, good brother; we shall thrive, I trust.

---

279. *a head* an army.
280. *even* calmly.
283. *pay us home* pay us in full; but note the association of
"home" with "home thrust"—a fatal blow.
289. *suddenly* very soon.

HOTSPUR

Uncle, adieu. O let the hours be short,
Till fields, and blows, and groans applaud our sport!

Exeunt.

[*Act II, scene i: Early the morning after Act I, scene ii, in an inn-yard at Rochester.*] *Enter a* Carrier *with a lantern in his hand.*

FIRST CARRIER

Heigh-ho! An' it be not four by the day, I'll be hanged;
Charles' Wain is over the new chimney, and yet our horse not
packed—what, ostler!

OSTLER [*offstage*]

Anon, anon.

FIRST CARRIER

5   I prithee, Tom, beat Cut's saddle, put a few flocks in the point
—poor jade is wrung in the withers out of all cess.

Enter another Carrier.

SECOND CARRIER

Peas and beans are as dank here as a dog, and that is the
next way to give poor jades the bots: this house is turned upside down since Robin Ostler died.

S.D. See I.ii.103*ff*.
1. *four by the day*   four o'clock in the morning.
2. *Charles' Wain*   the constellation now called the Plough or Dipper; the Latin name was *plaustrum*, (wagon or wain), and Kittredge suggests *Charles'* (Charlemagne's) is a corruption of *churl's* (peasant's). *horse* horses (see Appendix C, p. 168).
5. *beat . . . point*   Beating softened the leather; "Cut" suggests a pulling horse, with a docked tail; flocks are tufts of wool; the point is the saddle's pommel.
6. *wrung . . . cess*   chafed by harness on the ridge between the shoulder blades, excessively.
7. *peas and beans*   cheap substitute for oats.
8. *bots*   intestinal worms.

FIRST CARRIER

10   Poor fellow never joyed since the price of oats rose; it was the
death of him.

SECOND CARRIER

I think this be the most villainous house in all London road
for fleas, I am stung like a tench.

FIRST CARRIER

Like a tench?—by the mass, there is ne'er a king christen could
15   be better bit than I have been since the first cock.

SECOND CARRIER

Why, they will allow us ne'er a jordan, and then we leak in
your chimney, and your chamber-lye breeds fleas like a loach.

FIRST CARRIER

What, ostler! Come away and be hanged, come away!

SECOND CARRIER

I have a gammon of bacon, and two razes of ginger, to be de-
20   livered as far as Charing Cross.

FIRST CARRIER

God's body!—the turkeys in my pannier are quite starved—
what, ostler! A plague on thee, hast thou never an eye in thy
head? canst not hear? And 'twere not as good deed as drink
to break the pate on thee, I am a very villain. Come, and be
25   hanged! Hast no faith in thee?

---

13. *like a tench*   This fish's spotted markings suggest bites by parasites.

14. *by the mass*   a common mild oath. *king christen*   a Christian
king—Kittredge interprets this as assuming that kings always excel!

15. *first cock*   midnight (by convention).

16. *jordan*   chamber pot.

17. *chamber-lye*   urine. *loach*   a small and prolific river fish; use
of the word may be analogous to that of *tench* above.

19. *gammon*   bottom end of a side. *razes*   roots (archaic English
form of old French *rais*).

20. *Charing Cross*   then a village on the western side of London,
farthest from Rochester, which stands on the estuary east of the
capital.

Enter GADSHILL.

GADSHILL

Good morrow, carriers, what's o'clock?

[FIRST] CARRIER

I think it be two o'clock.

GADSHILL

I prithee lend me thy lantern, to see my gelding in the stable.

FIRST CARRIER

Nay, by God, soft! I know a trick worth two of that, i'faith.

GADSHILL

30   I pray thee, lend me thine.

SECOND CARRIER

Ay, when? Canst tell? "Lend me thy lantern," quoth he! Marry, I'll see thee hanged first.

GADSHILL

Sirrah carrier, what time do you mean to come to London?

SECOND CARRIER

Time enough to go to bed with a candle, I warrant thee . . .
35   come neighbour Mugs, we'll call up the gentlemen, they will along with company, for they have great charge.

Exeunt [Carriers].

GADSHILL

What ho! Chamberlain.

CHAMBERLAIN [*offstage*]

"At hand," quoth pickpurse.

GADSHILL [*aside*]

That's even as fair as " 'At hand,' quoth the chamberlain": for

---

29. *soft* Wait a moment. *trick* The carrier implies that Gadshill means to steal the lantern and claims he is more cunning than Gadshill.

34. *Time . . . candle* before daylight.

36. *great charge* much money or luggage to look after.

37. *Chamberlain* person in charge of inn's accommodation.

38. *At . . . pickpurse* a proverbial phrase, from the pickpocket's alertness, or closeness.

40   thou variest no more from picking of purses than giving direction doth from labouring: thou layest the plot how.

Enter Chamberlain.

CHAMBERLAIN

Good morrow, Master Gadshill. It holds current, that I told you yesternight: there's a franklin in the Weald of Kent hath brought three hundred marks with him in gold, I heard him
45   tell it to one of his company last night at supper—a kind of auditor, one that hath abundance of charge too, God knows what; they are up already, and call for eggs and butter—they will away presently.

GADSHILL

Sirrah, if they meet not with Saint Nicholas' clerks, I'll give
50   thee this neck.

CHAMBERLAIN

No, I'll none of it; I pray thee keep that for the hangman, for I know thou worshippest Saint Nicholas as truly as a man of falsehood may.

GADSHILL

What talkest thou to me of the hangman? If I hang, I'll make
55   a fat pair of gallows: for if I hang, old Sir John hangs with me,

---

41. *plot*   for a robbery. *S.D.*   at line 36 in Q1; but the Chamberlain greets Gadshill only at line 42 and seems not to have heard his abuse.

43. *franklin*   a landowner not of the nobility. *Weald*   Wild Qq— an appropriate corruption of the corrected reading; this is a rich, once wooded region in Sussex, Surrey, and Kent. Weald (compare *wold* and German *wald*) meant forest, but the name in England is limited to this particular area, originally called Andredsweald.

44. *marks*   The mark was valued at two-thirds of an English pound.

46. *auditor*   public accountant.

49. *Saint . . . clerks*   As patron of travelers and scholars, Saint Nicholas became popularly associated with vagabonds and, ultimately, with highwaymen (see O. E. Albrecht, *Four Latin Plays of St. Nicholas*). The analogy to "Old Nick" (the devil) may have helped.

and thou knowest he is no starveling. Tut, there are other
Troyans that thou dream'st not of, the which for sport sake
are content to do the profession some grace, that would (if
matters should be looked into) for their own credit sake make
60 all whole. I am joined with no foot-landrakers, no long-staff
sixpenny strikers, none of these mad mustachio purple-hued
maltworms, but with nobility, and tranquillity, burgomasters
and great one-ers, such as can hold in, such as will strike sooner
than speak, and speak sooner than drink, and drink sooner
65 than pray—and yet, 'zounds, I lie, for they pray continually to
their saint of Commonwealth, or rather not pray to her, but
prey on her, for they ride up and down on her, and make her
their boots.

CHAMBERLAIN

What, the Commonwealth their boots? Will she hold out water
70 in foul way?

GADSHILL

She will, she will—Justice hath liquored her: we steal as in a

---

57. *Troyans* used (like *Corinthian*, II.iv.10) for roisterers.

60–62. *foot-landrakers* vagabond thieves. *long-staff sixpenny
strikers* thieves armed with staves who will rob for sixpence. *mustachio . . . maltworms* drinkers of beer (made with malt) whose top-
ing has stained their moustaches purple. *tranquillity* those who live
at ease.

63. *great one-ers* great oneyers Qq—though much debated by editors (who made conjectures like Malone's *onyers*: fiscal officials; Capell's *mynheers*; Collier's *ones*; *-yes*, etc.), this phrase is, most probably, a slangy variant of *great ones*, as *-er* is a common suffix to
identify a person's profession, status, origins, etc.; compare *land-
rakers, strikers, burgomasters*. In this sense, Lettsom noted that *one-
er* appears in Dickens' *Old Curiosity Shop*, Ch.LVIII, in slang dialogue.

68. *boots* in the sense of booty or spoil.

71. *liquored* Kittredge quotes *The Return from Parnassus*, III.i:
"The liquoring of boots for the holding out of water." But such "greas-
ing" had probably the modern overtone of bribery also; and the
simpler sense of "Justice" intoxicating or debauching the Commonwealth is valid.

castle, cocksure; we have the receipt of fernseed, we walk invisible.

CHAMBERLAIN

Nay by my faith, I think you are more beholding to the night
75 than to fernseed for your walking invisible.

GADSHILL

Give me thy hand—thou shalt share in our purchase, as I am
a true man.

CHAMBERLAIN

Nay, rather let me have it, "as you are a false thief."

GADSHILL

Go to, *homo* is a common name to all men. Bid the ostler bring
80 my gelding out of the stable. Farewell, you muddy knave.

[*Exeunt.*]

[*Scene ii: Later that morning at Gad's Hill, on the road to
London.*] *Enter* PRINCE, POINS, *and* PETO.

POINS

Come, shelter, shelter! I have removed Falstaff's horse, and he
frets like a gummed velvet.

71–2. *in a castle*   in complete safety. *receipt of fernseed*   The formula for invisibility was to carry fernseed, which was visible and was
gathered only on Midsummer Day (June 23).

76. *purchase*   ironic word for loot; often contrasted with legitimate
inheritance in Elizabethan usage: "For what in me was purchased,/
Falls upon thee in a more fairer sort" (*2HIV*, IV.v.200–1).

79. *homo*   Gadshill claims that by "as I am a true man" he merely
meant "as I am accurately defined as man" (whether a false or a trustworthy one) and thus may repudiate the chamberlain's epithet, since
the category *homo* covers all kinds of individual men.

S.D. PETO   *Peto, &c.* Qq—"etc." may refer to Falstaff's almost immediate entry. Bardolph most probably enters with Gadshill at line 39.

2. *gummed velvet*   Cheap velvet needed gum to stiffen it and give
a good surface, but it then wore (or "fretted") very readily—hence the
analogy to Falstaff's temper.

37

PRINCE

Stand close.

[*They draw back to watch.*]

Enter FALSTAFF.

FALSTAFF

Poins! Poins, and be hanged! Poins!

PRINCE [*coming forward*]

5   Peace ye fat-kidneyed rascal, what a brawling dost thou keep!

FALSTAFF

Where's Poins, Hal?

PRINCE

He is walked up to the top of the hill; I'll go seek him.

[*He retires again.*]

FALSTAFF

I am accursed to rob in that thief's company: the rascal hath
removed my horse and tied him I know not where. If I travel
10   but four foot by the squier further afoot, I shall break my
wind. Well, I doubt not but to die a fair death for all this, if I
'scape hanging for killing that rogue. I have forsworn his company hourly any time this two-and-twenty years, and yet I am
bewitched with the rogue's company. If the rascal have not
15   given me medicines to make me love him, I'll be hanged. It
could not be else, I have drunk medicines. Poins! Hal! A plague
upon you both! Bardolph! Peto! I'll **starve** e'er I'll rob a foot

---

3. *close*   close to cover, for concealment.

8ff. Craig's edn. quotes Nashe's "The Complaint of Gluttony" in
Piers Peniless (McKerrow's edn., I, 201) as a source for this detail:
"The Roman Censors, if they lighted upon a fat corpulent man, they
straight took away his horse, and constrained him to go a foot: . . . If
we had such horse-takers amongst us . . . surfeit-swolne churls, who
now ride on foot-cloths might be constrained to carry their flesh on
foot . . . and the price of velvet and cloth would fall with their bellies!"

10. *by the squier*   Falstaff measures his walking with a carpenter's
square, or measure.

15. *medicines*   love potions.

17. *starve*   die (the archaic meaning of the verb).

further—and 'twere not as good a deed as drink to turn true
man, and to leave these rogues, I am the veriest varlet that ever
20   chewed with a tooth: eight yards of uneven ground is threescore and ten miles afoot with me, and the stony-hearted villains know it well enough. A plague upon it when thieves cannot be true one to another. (*They whistle.*) Whew! A plague
upon you all, give me my horse you rogues, give me my horse
25   and be hanged!

PRINCE [*coming forward*]

Peace, ye fat guts; lie down, lay thine ear close to the ground,
and list if thou canst hear the tread of travellers.

FALSTAFF

Have you any levers to lift me up again being down? 'Sblood,
I'll not bear mine own flesh so far afoot again for all the coin
30   in thy father's exchequer. What a plague mean ye to colt me
thus?

PRINCE

Thou liest—thou art not colted, thou art uncolted.

FALSTAFF

I prithee good Prince Hal, help me to my horse, good king's
son.

PRINCE

35   Out, ye rogue, shall I be your ostler?

FALSTAFF

Hang thyself in thine own heir-apparent garters! If I be ta'en,
I'll peach for this. And I have not ballads made on you all, and
sung to filthy tunes, let a cup of sack be my poison. When a

---

18. *true*   honest.
19. *varlet*   rascal.
30. *colt*   trick.
35. *Out*   away with you.
36. *heir-apparent garters*   The heir to the throne is enrolled in the
Order of the Garter.
37. *peach*   give information to the authorities.

jest is so forward—and afoot too—I hate it.

Enter GADSHILL [*and* BARDOLPH].

GADSHILL

40   Stand!

FALSTAFF

So I do, against my will.

POINS [*coming forward with* PETO]

O, 'tis our setter, I know his voice. Bardolph, what news?

BARDOLPH

Case ye, case ye, on with your vizards—there's money of the
king's coming down the hill, 'tis going to the king's exchequer.

FALSTAFF

45   You lie, ye rogue! 'Tis going to the King's Tavern.

GADSHILL

There's enough to make us all . . .

FALSTAFF

To be hanged.

PRINCE

Sirs, you four shall front them in the narrow lane; Ned Poins
and I will walk lower—if they 'scape from your encounter,
50   then they light on us.

PETO

How many be there of them?

GADSHILL

Some eight or ten.

FALSTAFF

'Zounds, will they not rob us?

---

39. *forward*   excessive.

39. [*and* BARDOLPH]   not in QqF.; but the question at line 42
makes clear that he must enter with Gadshill.

42. *setter*   arranger of robberies (compare setter dog, which indicates game to hunters).

43. *case*   mask.

46. *make us all . . .*   "rich" is understood, though Falstaff concludes
differently.

PRINCE

What, a coward, Sir John Paunch?

FALSTAFF

55   Indeed I am not John of Gaunt, your grandfather, but yet no
coward, Hal.

PRINCE

Well, we leave that to the proof.

POINS

Sirrah Jack, thy horse stands behind the hedge; when thou
need'st him, there thou shalt find him. Farewell, and stand fast.

FALSTAFF

60   Now cannot I strike him, if I should be hanged.

PRINCE [*aside*]

Ned, where are our disguises?

POINS [*aside*]

Here, hard by; stand close.

[*Exeunt* PRINCE *and* POINS.]

FALSTAFF

Now my masters, happy man be his dole, say I—every man to
his business.

Enter the Travellers.

TRAVELLER

65   Come neighbour, the boy shall lead our horses down the hill;
we'll walk afoot awhile and ease our legs.

THIEVES

Stand!

TRAVELLER

Jesus bless us!

---

55. *John of Gaunt*   the famous Duke of Lancaster and Hal's grandfather; his name comes from his birthplace, Ghent, but perhaps Falstaff implies an allusion to the thin (of "gaunt") physique characteristic to members of the House of Lancaster (see II.iv.210ff.).
    63. *happy . . . dole*   may each man be happy in his destiny ("dole"
is dealt out by Fate).

FALSTAFF

Strike!—down with them!—cut the villains' throats! Ah,
70 whoreson caterpillars, bacon-fed knaves, they hate us youth!
Down with them!—fleece them!

TRAVELLER

O, we are undone, both we and ours forever!

FALSTAFF

Hang ye, gorbellied knaves, are ye undone? No, ye fat chuffs;
I would your store were here! On, bacons, on! What, ye
75 knaves?—young men must live! You are grandjurors are ye?
—we'll jure ye, 'faith.
                              Here they rob them and bind them. Exeunt.

                    [Re-]enter the PRINCE *and* POINS *[disguised].*

PRINCE

The thieves have bound the true men; now could thou and I
rob the thieves, and go merrily to London, it would be argument for a week, laughter for a month, and a good jest forever.

POINS

80 Stand close, I hear them coming.   *[They stand back.]*

                    Enter the Thieves *again.*

FALSTAFF

Come my masters, let us share, and then to horse before day.
And the Prince and Poins be not two arrant cowards there's

69–71. Falstaff's shouted abuse is intended to unnerve the travellers. He accuses them of his own faults: *caterpillars* are parasites; *gorbellied* means fat-paunched; *chuffs* are rustic boors, or churls—but
OED notes that the word is often used with allusion to *chough*: a kind
of crow—originally applied to noisy (and thieving) birds, especially
jackdaws.

75. *grandjurors* Prosperous citizens served on grand juries.

76. *jure* Such meaningless repetition is common in humorous
threats.

78–9. *argument* subject for discussion.

no equity stirring; there's no more valour in that Poins than in
a wild duck.

> *As they are sharing, the* PRINCE *and* POINS *set upon them.*

PRINCE

85 Your money!

POINS

Villains!

> *They all run away, and* FALSTAFF *after a blow or two*
> *runs away too, leaving the booty behind them.*

PRINCE

Got with much ease. Now merrily to horse:
The thieves are all scattered and possessed with fear
So strongly that they dare not meet each other,
90 Each takes his fellow for an officer.
Away, good Ned! Falstaff sweats to death,
And lards the lean earth as he walks along—
Were't not for laughing, I should pity him.

POINS

How the fat rogue roared.

> *Exeunt.*

[*Scene iii: Some time after I.ii, at Warkworth Castle.*] *Enter*
HOTSPUR *alone, reading a letter.*

HOTSPUR

". . . but for mine own part, my lord, I could be well contented
to be there, in respect of the love I bear your house." He could
be contented—why is he not then? In respect of the love

---

83. *no equity stirring* no good judgment being practiced.

87–93. These lines appear as prose in QqF, but blank verse normally emphasizes Hal's status at scene-ends.

94. *fat* Qq omit this word; the fragment of the otherwise lost
earliest quarto (Q0) alone includes it.

S.D. *Warkworth Castle* home of the Percys, in Northumberland.

2. *house* family.

he bears our house! He shows in this he loves his own barn
5	better than he loves our house. Let me see some more. "The
purpose you undertake is dangerous." Why that's certain; 'tis
dangerous to take a cold, to sleep, to drink; but I tell you, my
Lord Fool, out of this nettle, danger, we pluck this flower,
safety. "The purpose you undertake is dangerous, the friends
10	you have named uncertain, the time itself unsorted, and your
whole plot too light for the counterpoise of so great an opposition." Say you so, say you so? I say unto you again, you are a
shallow cowardly hind, and you lie: what a lack-brain is this!
By the Lord, our plot is a good plot as ever was laid, our friends
15	true and constant: a good plot, good friends, and full of ex-
pectation; an excellent plot, very good friends—what a frosty-
spirited rogue is this! Why, my Lord of York commends the
plot, and the general course of the action. 'Zounds, and I were
now by this rascal I could brain him with his lady's fan. Is
20	there not my father, my uncle, and myself; Lord Edmund
Mortimer, my Lord of York, and Owen Glendower; is there
not besides the Douglas; have I not all their letters to meet me
in arms by the ninth of the next month, and are they not some
of them set forward already? What a pagan rascal is this, an in-
25	fidel! Ha! You shall see now in very sincerity of fear and cold
heart will he to the king, and lay open all our proceedings! O,
I could divide myself, and go to buffets, for moving such a dish
of skim milk with so honorable an action. Hang him, let him
tell the king—we are prepared: I will set forward tonight.

Enter his Lady.

30	How now, Kate? I must leave you within these two hours.

---

10. *unsorted*	ill-chosen.

13. *hind*	peasant.

24. *pagan*	lacking faith.

27. *divide . . . buffets*	divide myself physically and set both parts
to hitting each other.

30. *Kate*	historically named Elizabeth; Holinshed changes her to
"Elianor," and Shakespeare renames her Kate, a name he favors for
his heroines (see *Shrew, HV*).

LADY PERCY

O my good lord, why are you thus alone?
For what offence have I this fortnight been
A banished woman from my Harry's bed?
Tell me, sweet lord, what is't that takes from thee
35   Thy stomach, pleasure, and thy golden sleep?
Why dost thou bend thine eyes upon the earth,
And start so often when thou sit'st alone?
Why hast thou lost the fresh blood in thy cheeks,
And given my treasures and my rights of thee
40   To thick-eyed musing and curst melancholy?
In thy faint slumbers I by thee have watched,
And heard thee murmur tales of iron wars,
Speak terms of manage to thy bounding steed,
Cry "Courage! To the field!" And thou hast talked
45   Of sallies and retires, of trenches, tents,
Of palisadoes, frontiers, parapets,
Of basilisks, of cannon, culverin,
Of prisoners' ransom, and of soldiers slain,
And all the currents of a heady fight.
50   Thy spirit within thee hath been so at war,
And thus hath so bestirred thee in thy sleep,
That beads of sweat have stood upon thy brow
Like bubbles in a late-disturbèd stream,
And in thy face strange motions have appeared,
55   Such as we see when men restrain their breath,
On some great sudden hest. O, what portents are these?

---

35. *stomach*   appetite.

40. *thick-eyed musing*   preoccupations that impair visual alertness.

43. *manage*   manège, horsemanship.

46. *palisadoes*   a line of pointed stakes, originally a defense against cavalry. *frontiers*   outworks of fortifications.

47. *basilisks . . . culverin*   The basilisk was the largest cannon of the day (named after a mythical monster that turned men to stone by its look, or breath); the culverin, the smallest (compare Fr. *couleuvre*, **adder**).

56. *hest*   behest, order.

Some heavy business hath my lord in hand,
And I must know it, else he loves me not.

HOTSPUR

What ho!

[*Enter a* Servant.]

Is Gilliams with the packet gone?

SERVANT

60   He is, my lord, an hour ago.

HOTSPUR

Hath Butler brought those horses from the sheriff?

SERVANT

One horse, my lord, he brought even now.

HOTSPUR

What horse? A roan, a crop-ear is it not?

SERVANT

It is, my lord.

HOTSPUR

That roan shall be my throne.
65   Well, I will back him straight. "O Esperance!"
Bid Butler lead him forth into the park.   [*Exit* Servant.]

LADY PERCY

But hear you, my lord.

HOTSPUR

What say'st thou, my lady?

LADY PERCY

What is it carries you away?

---

63. *horse. A roan*   horse, a roane Q3–5,F. horse, Roane? Q1,2.
roan   dappled color.

65. *Esperance*   Kittredge notes that the motto of the Percys is "Esperance ma conforte" ("Hope is my stay") and compares this with V.ii.96.

69. *carries you away*   She means "excites you"; Hotspur pretends to take it literally.

HOTSPUR

70   Why, my horse, my love, my horse.

LADY PERCY

Out, you mad-headed ape!
A weasel hath not such a deal of spleen
As you are tossed with. In faith,
I'll know your business, Harry, that I will!
75   I fear my brother Mortimer doth stir
About his title, and hath sent for you
To line his enterprise; but if you go . . .

HOTSPUR

So far afoot, I shall be weary, love.

LADY PERCY

Come, come, you paraquito, answer me
80   Directly unto this question that I ask;
In faith, I'll break thy little finger, Harry,
And if thou wilt not tell me all things true.

HOTSPUR

Away, away you trifler! Love, I love thee not—
I care not for thee, Kate; this is no world
85   To play with mammets, and to tilt with lips;

---

72. *spleen*   This organ was supposed to govern abrupt reactions, and came to stand for "excitability."

75. *brother Mortimer*   This Mortimer was historically her nephew.

77. *line*   reinforce.

79. *paraquito*   early form (It. or Span.?) of "parakeet"—a small parrot, noisy and brightly colored.

81. *thy little finger*   "No sorts of kisses or follies in love were forgotten, . . . no pinching by the little finger," G. Fenton, *Tragical Discourses*, 1567 (Tudor Translations ii,102). Lady Percy's concern and affection cause her to switch from the more formal "you" and "your" to the intimate "thou" and "thy," as does Hotspur later. See Appendix C, p. 169.

85. *mammets*   dolls.

We must have bloody noses, and cracked crowns,
And pass them current too. God s'me, my horse!
What say'st thou Kate? What would'st thou have with me?

LADY PERCY

Do you not love me? Do you not indeed?
90   Well, do not then; for since you love me not
I will not love, myself. Do you not love me?
Nay, tell me if you speak in jest or no?

HOTSPUR

Come, wilt thou see me ride? . . .
And when I am a-horseback I will swear
95   I love thee infinitely. But hark you, Kate,
I must not have you henceforth question me
Whither I go, nor reason whereabout;
Whither I must, I must; and to conclude—
This evening must I leave you, gentle Kate.
100   I know you wise, but yet no farther wise
Than Harry Percy's wife; constant you are,
But yet a woman; and for secrecy
No lady closer, for I well believe
Thou wilt not utter what thou dost not know,
105   And so far will I trust thee, gentle Kate.

LADY PERCY

How?—so far?

HOTSPUR

Not an inch further. But hark you, Kate—

86–7. *cracked . . . current*   A cracked coin was not supposed to be acceptable currency—hence the word-play.

87. *God s'me*   God save me.

91. *love, myself*   love myself QqF, which reads too solemnly to match Hotspur's teasing.

102–5. *woman . . . trust*   proverbial masculine opinions from antiquity; compare Seneca, *Controversiae*, II.xiii.12: "do not commit important information to a garrulous woman, who will only conceal what she does not know."

Whither I go, thither shall you go too:
Today will I set forth, tomorrow you.
Will this content you, Kate?

                    LADY PERCY
110   It must, of force.

                                        Exeunt.

[*Scene iv: The evening after the robbery, at the Boar's Head
Tavern in Eastcheap.*] *Enter* PRINCE *and* POINS.

                    PRINCE

Ned, prithee, come out of that fat-room, and lend me thy hand
to laugh a little.

                    POINS

Where hast been, Hal?

                    PRINCE

With three or four loggerheads, amongst three or four score
5   hogsheads. I have sounded the very base-string of humility.
Sirrah, I am sworn brother to a leash of drawers, and can call
them all by their christen names, as Tom, Dick, and Francis.
They take it already upon their salvation, that though I be but
Prince of Wales, yet I am the King of Courtesy, and tell me
10   flatly I am no proud Jack like Falstaff, but a Corinthian, a lad

---

110. *of force*   perforce.
S.D. *at . . . Eastcheap*   *2HIV*, II.ii.140–2 suggests the name of this
well-known tavern as the locale of Falstaff's escapades; Hal has already planned to meet Falstaff in Eastcheap (see I.ii.158). Of course,
the original text does not identify the setting.
1. *fat-room*   either a stuffy room, or the vat-room (vat was originally spelt "fat") where beer was stored, or fermented. As Hal appears
just to have left the latter, the former meaning is likely.
4. *loggerheads*   blockheads.
6. *leash*   three, a hunting term (compare *brace*, two).
10. *Jack*   could mean *fellow*, as well as alluding to Falstaff's Christian name.   *Corinthian*   a gay companion; an allusion to Corinth's
reputation for luxury in classical times.

of mettle, a good boy (by the Lord, so they call me!) and when
I am King of England I shall command all the good lads in
Eastcheap. They call drinking deep "dyeing scarlet," and when
you breathe in your watering they cry "Hem!" and bid you
15   "Play it off!" To conclude, I am so good a proficient in one
quarter of an hour that I can drink with any tinker in his own
language during my life. I tell thee, Ned, thou hast lost much
honour that thou wert not with me in this action; but sweet
Ned—to sweeten which name of Ned, I give thee this penny-
20   worth of sugar, clapped even now into my hand by an under-
skinker, one that never spake other English in his life than
"Eight shillings and sixpence," and "You are welcome," with
this shrill addition, "Anon, anon, sir! . . . Score a pint of bastard in the Half Moon," or so. But, Ned, to drive away the time
25   till Falstaff come—I prithee do thou stand in some by-room,
while I question my puny drawer to what end he gave me the
sugar, and do thou never leave calling "Francis!" that his tale

---

13. *dyeing scarlet*   acquiring a flushed complexion, like Bardolph's.
Urine was used in making scarlet dyes.
14–15. *breathe in your watering*   The practiced drinker drains his
tankard without stopping for breath; "watering" was slang for drinking (compare watering a horse). *Hem*   clearing one's throat is often
a sign of criticism but is sometimes meant as encouragement—in
2HIV, III.ii.212–3, Shallow recalls that, in his youth, "Our watchword
was 'Hem, boy!'" *Play it off*   drink it off.
16. *tinker*   Overbury observes in his *Characters* that the tinker
goes "where the best Ale is" and "is very voluble."
18. *action*   encounter, usually military.
20–21. *sugar*   used to sweeten wine. *under-skinker*   under-tapster;
to skink is to pour or draw wine, etc.
23. *Anon*   Originally, this meant "at once" (as did *presently*).
23–4. *bastard*   a Spanish wine, so-called because it was adulterated
with sugar. *Half Moon*   the name of the room to whose reckoning
the cost of the wine was to be added. Rooms were named, not num-
bered, in inns; compare *Pomgarnet*, line 32.

to me may be nothing but "Anon." Step aside and I'll show
thee a precedent . . .

POINS

30   Francis!

PRINCE

Thou art perfect! [POINS *withdraws.*] Francis!

Enter [FRANCIS, *a*] *drawer.*

FRANCIS

Anon, anon, sir. Look down into the Pomgarnet, Ralph.

PRINCE

Come hither, Francis.

FRANCIS

My lord?

PRINCE

35   How long hast thou to serve, Francis?

FRANCIS

Forsooth, five years, and as much as to . . .

POINS [*offstage*]

Francis!

FRANCIS

Anon, anon, sir.

PRINCE

Five year!—by'r Lady, a long lease for the clinking of pewter;
40   but Francis, darest thou be so valiant as to play the coward
with thy indenture, and show it a fair pair of heels, and run
from it?

---

29. *precedent*   F. present Qq. A precedent was an example.

32. *Pomgarnet*   an archaism for pomegranate. See note, line 24.

35. *serve*   as apprentice, Francis would have to spend a total of
seven years learning his trade.

39. *long lease*   a long contract (to learn how to handle pewter
mugs).

40–41. *play . . . indenture*   break your contract with your employer.

FRANCIS

O Lord, sir, I'll be sworn upon all the books in England, I could find in my heart . . .

POINS [*offstage*]

45   Francis!

FRANCIS

Anon, sir.

PRINCE

How old art thou, Francis?

FRANCIS

Let me see, about Michaelmas next I shall be . . .

POINS [*offstage*]

Francis!

FRANCIS

50   Anon, sir—pray stay a little, my lord.

PRINCE

Nay, but hark you, Francis, for the sugar thou gavest me—
'twas a pennyworth, was't not? . . .

FRANCIS

O Lord, I would it had been two!

PRINCE

I will give thee for it a thousand pound: ask me when thou
55   wilt and thou shalt have it.

POINS [*offstage*]

Francis!

FRANCIS

Anon, anon.

PRINCE

Anon, Francis? No, Francis, but tomorrow, Francis; or, Francis,

---

43. *books* Bibles.
48. *Michaelmas* September 29, the day honoring the Archangel Michael; an important holiday, marking an accounting period in business.

a'Thursday; or indeed, Francis, when thou wilt. But, Francis!...

FRANCIS

60   My lord?

PRINCE

Wilt thou rob this leathern-jerkin, crystal-button, not-pated, agate-ring, puke-stocking, caddis-garter, smooth-tongue Spanish-pouch?

FRANCIS

O Lord, sir, who do you mean?

PRINCE

65   Why then your brown bastard is your only drink: for look you, Francis, your white canvas doublet will sully. In Barbary, sir, it cannot come to so much.

FRANCIS

What, sir?

POINS [*offstage*]

Francis!

PRINCE

70   Away, you rogue, dost thou not hear them call?
          [FRANCIS *starts to leave;*] *here they both call him* [*alter-nately, and*] *the drawer* [*tries to run both ways; at last he*] *stands amazed not knowing which way to go. Enter* Vintner.

61–3. *Wilt . . . pouch*   because of Francis' wasting of the sugar, or his desire to leave the inn. The Prince appears to question Francis' loyalty to his employer, who is described somewhat satirically, as wearing a leather jacket, with crystal buttons; having his hair crew-cut (*not-pated*); with an agate in his ring (a carved stone often used as a seal); his stockings were dark colored wool, which was ungentle-manly, as was the use of cheap tape (*caddis*) for garters, instead of silk. Spanish leather is a famous material for money pouches such as the innkeeper wore.

65. *your*   No specific reference to Francis is intended—throughout this speech Hal is speaking at random to confuse Francis.

67. *it*   The prince is thinking of the sugar perhaps, which was pro-duced in Barbary. Kittredge says Hal is suggesting Francis will end

VINTNER

What, stand'st thou still and hear'st such a calling? Look to the guests within. [*Exit* FRANCIS.] My lord, old Sir John with half-a-dozen more are at the door—shall I let them in?

PRINCE

Let them alone awhile, and then open the door. [*Exit* Vintner.]
75 Poins!

[*Re-]enter* POINS.

POINS

Anon, anon, sir.

PRINCE

Sirrah, Falstaff and the rest of the thieves are at the door; shall we be merry?

POINS

As merry as crickets, my lad—but hark ye, what cunning
80 match have you made with this jest of the drawer: come, what's the issue?

PRINCE

I am now of all humours that have showed themselves humours since the old days of goodman Adam to the pupil age of this present twelve o'clock at midnight.

[FRANCIS *crosses the stage.*]
85 What's o'clock, Francis?

FRANCIS

Anon, anon, sir.

[*Exit* FRANCIS.]

PRINCE

That ever this fellow should have fewer words than a parrot,

---

there if he "sullies his apron" by theft or flight, the "it" being his use-less apron.

79–80. *cunning match* clever game.

82. *all humours* The Prince feels relaxed and "free to indulge any fancy man has ever had" (Kittredge).

54

and yet the son of a woman! His industry is up-stairs and
down-stairs, his eloquence the parcel of a reckoning. I am not
90 yet of Percy's mind, the Hotspur of the North, he that kills
me some six or seven dozen of Scots at a breakfast, washes his
hands, and says to his wife, "Fie upon this quiet life, I want
work." "O my sweet Harry," says she, "how many hast thou
killed today?" "Give my roan horse a drench," says he, and
95 answers "Some fourteen" an hour after—"a trifle, a trifle." I
prithee call in Falstaff, I'll play Percy, and that damned brawn
shall play Dame Mortimer his wife. "Rivo!" says the drunkard:
call in Ribs, call in Tallow.

Enter FALSTAFF [, GADSHILL, BARDOLPH *and* PETO; FRANCIS
follows with wine.]

POINS

Welcome, Jack, where hast thou been?

FALSTAFF

100 A plague of all cowards, I say, and a vengeance too, marry and
amen! Give me a cup of sack, boy. Ere I lead this life long, I'll
sew nether-stocks and mend them and foot them too. A plague
of all cowards! Give me a cup of sack, rogue; is there no virtue
extant?

He drinketh.

PRINCE

105 Didst thou never see Titan kiss a dish of butter—pitiful
hearted Titan—that melted at the sweet tale of the Sun's? If
thou didst, then behold that compound.

---

89. *parcel . . . reckoning* details in a bill. Francis' factualness re-
minds Hal next of Hotspur's supposed curtness (see III.i.152–4).

94. *drench* dose of medicine.

97. *Rivo* The origin of this drinking cry is unknown, but it may
be Spanish: the *OED* suggests *arriba*, up (compare "bottoms up").

100. *marry* a vague kind of affirmative interjection, derived from
the name of the Virgin Mary.

102. *nether-stocks* stockings.

105–6. *Didst . . . Sun's* Hal compares the disappearing liquor and

FALSTAFF

You rogue, here's lime in this sack too: there is nothing but roguery to be found in villainous man, yet a coward is worse
110   than a cup of sack with lime in it. A villainous coward! Go thy ways, old Jack; die when thou wilt, if manhood, good manhood, be not forgot upon the face of the earth, then am I a shotten herring: there lives not three good men unhanged in England, and one of them is fat, and grows old. God help the
115   while! A bad world, I say, I would I were a weaver—I could sing psalms, or anything. A plague of all cowards, I say still.

PRINCE

How now, woolsack, what mutter you?

FALSTAFF

A king's son!—if I do not beat thee out of thy kingdom with a dagger of lath, and drive all thy subjects afore thee like a
120   flock of wild geese, I'll never wear hair on my face more—you, Prince of Wales!

PRINCE

Why, you whoreson round man, what's the matter?

FALSTAFF

Are not you a coward? Answer me to that—and Poins there?

---

the flushed face of Falstaff (together making "that compound") to a dish of butter melted by the loving attention of the sun ("Titan").

110. *lime*   a trick to give a dry flavor and sparkle to poor wine.

113. *shotten*   having discharged its roe.

114–15. *the while*   these times.

115. *weaver*   R. P. Cowl's *Sources of . . . Henry IV* quotes D'Avenant's *The Wits* (1636) I.i.84–7: "She is more devout/ Than a weaver of Banbury, that hopes/ T'entice Heaven, by singing, to make him lord/ Of Twenty looms." Some weavers came from the strongly Protestant Low Countries.

118–19. *beat . . . lath*   characteristic behavior of the comic Vice in the morality plays and interludes: "the old Vice . . ./ Who with dagger of lath,/ In his rage and his wrath/ Cries 'Ah, ha!' to the devil" (*TN*, IV.ii.134*ff.*).

POINS

'Zounds, ye fat paunch, and ye call me coward, by the Lord, I'll
125 stab thee.

FALSTAFF

I call thee coward? I'll see thee damned ere I call thee coward,
but I would give a thousand pound I could run as fast as thou
canst. You are straight enough in the shoulders, you care not
who sees your back: call you that backing of your friends? A
130 plague upon such backing; give me them that will face me!
Give me a cup of sack—I am a rogue if I drunk today.

PRINCE

O villain!—thy lips are scarce wiped since thou drunk'st last.

FALSTAFF

All is one for that. (*He drinketh.*) A plague of all cowards still,
say I.

PRINCE

135 What's the matter?

FALSTAFF

What's the matter? There be four of us here, have ta'en a thousand pound this day morning.

PRINCE

Where is it, Jack, where is it?

FALSTAFF

Where is it? Taken from us it is—a hundred upon poor four
140 of us.

PRINCE

What, a hundred, man?

FALSTAFF

I am a rogue if I were not at half-sword with a dozen of them
two hours together. I have 'scaped by miracle. I am eight times
thrust through the doublet, four through the hose, my buckler

---

133. *All . . . that* That makes no difference.
142. *at half-sword* at half a sword's length; i.e., closely.

145 cut through and through, my sword hacked like a handsaw—
ecce signum! I never dealt better since I was a man—all would
not do. A plague of all cowards! Let them speak; if they speak
more or less than truth, they are villains and the sons of darkness.

[PRINCE]

150 Speak, sirs, how was it?

[GADSHILL]

We four set upon some dozen . . .

FALSTAFF

Sixteen at least, my lord.

[GADSHILL]

And bound them.

PETO

No, no, they were not bound.

FALSTAFF

155 You rogue, they were bound, every man of them, or I am a
Jew else: an Ebrew Jew.

[GADSHILL]

As we were sharing, some six or seven fresh men set upon
us . . .

FALSTAFF

And unbound the rest, and then come in the other.

PRINCE

160 What, fought you with them all?

---

146. *ecce signum*   behold the sign; i.e., look at the evidence.
150–58. Qq give the Prince's inquiry to Gadshill, and Gadshill's
three speeches to Ross[ill]—presumably either an actor's name or one
surviving uncorrected from the Oldcastle version of the play (see note
on I.ii.133). The revised distribution of speeches adopted in F is traditionally accepted, as here. *NCS* suggests the Q1 compositor corrected
the wrong name, giving Gadshill the Prince's speech instead of Rossill's lines.
159. *other*   others (such apparently singular nouns were commonly
used in a plural sense; see p. 168).

FALSTAFF

All? I know not what you call all, but if I fought not with fifty of them I am a bunch of radish: if there were not two or three and fifty upon poor old Jack, then am I no two-legged creature.

PRINCE

Pray God you have not murdered some of them.

FALSTAFF

165   Nay, that's past praying for—I have peppered two of them. Two I am sure I have paid, two rogues in buckram suits. I tell thee what, Hal, if I tell thee a lie, spit in my face, call me horse. Thou knowest my old ward: here I lay, and thus I bore my point—four rogues in buckram let drive at me. . . .

PRINCE

170   What four?—thou said'st but two even now.

FALSTAFF

Four, Hal, I told thee four.

POINS

Ay, ay, he said four.

FALSTAFF

These four came all afront, and mainly thrust at me; I made me no more ado, but took all their seven points in my target,
175   thus.

PRINCE

Seven!—why there were but four even now.

---

162. *radish*   Wilson's edn. notes that radishes were associated with slimness: "Radish roots have the vertue to extenuate or make thin" (T. Elyot, *Castle of Health*, 1534).

166. *paid*   settled with; i.e., killed.

167. *horse*   often considered a stupid animal: "A very horse, that has he knows not what" (*T&C*, III.iii.127–7).

168. *ward*   defensive posture in sword fighting. *here I lay* thus I stood.

173. *afront* abreast. *mainly* strongly.

174. *target*   a kind of shield, here used as equivalent to "buckler," though technically the target was heavier.

FALSTAFF

In buckram?

POINS

Ay, four in buckram suits.

FALSTAFF

Seven, by these hilts, or I am a villain else.

PRINCE [aside to POINS]

180 Prithee let him alone—we shall have more anon.

FALSTAFF

Dost thou hear me, Hal?

PRINCE

Ay, and mark thee too, Jack.

FALSTAFF

Do so, for it is worth the listening to—these nine in buckram
that I told thee of . . .

PRINCE [to POINS]

185 So, two more already.

FALSTAFF

. . . their points being broken . . .

POINS

Down fell their hose.

FALSTAFF

. . . began to give me ground; but I followed me close, came in,
foot and hand, and with a thought, seven of the eleven I paid.

PRINCE

190 O monstrous!—eleven buckram men grown out of two!

---

179. *hilts* plural because made of several parts; the cross formed
by a sword handle made it something upon which to take an oath (see
Ham, I.v.147).

182. *mark* a pun: to mark meant to keep score, as well as to pay
attention.

186–7. *points . . . hose* a play on the two meanings of "points"—
sword points, and the laces attaching one's hose to his doublet.

188. *give me . . . followed me* reflexive dative (see p. 168).

FALSTAFF

But as the Devil would have it, three misbegotten knaves in
Kendal green came at my back and let drive at me; for it was
so dark, Hal, that thou couldest not see thy hand.

PRINCE

These lies are like their father that begets them, gross as a
195 mountain, open, palpable. Why thou clay-brained guts, thou
knotty-pated fool, thou whoreson obscene greasy tallow-
catch . . .

FALSTAFF

What, art thou mad? art thou mad? Is not the truth the truth?

PRINCE

Why, how couldst thou know these men in Kendal green when
200 it was so dark thou couldst not see thy hand? Come, tell us
your reason. What sayest thou to this?

POINS

Come, your reason, Jack, your reason.

FALSTAFF

What, upon compulsion? 'Zounds, and I were at the strappado,
or all the racks in the world, I would not tell you on compul-
205 sion. Give you a reason on compulsion? If reasons were as
plentiful as blackberries, I would give no man a reason upon
compulsion, I.

---

192. *Kendal green* The coarse cloth so named was made in Kendal,
in Westmoreland. It was worn by woodsmen (and possibly by such figures as Robin Hood and his men).

196. *knotty-pated* blockheaded.

196–7. *tallow-catch* either a receptacle for fat drippings from a
roast, or (according to Kittredge) "a variant of tallow-keech": a lump
of tallow rolled up by butchers for candle-making.

203. *strappado* a device of torture. Steevens' edn. quotes R.
Holmes's *Academy of Armory and Blazon*, 1688, III.310: "to have the
man's arms tied cross behind his back, and so by them to be drawn up
to a considerable height and so let down again"—sometimes this was
done with a jerk that broke the arms.

205. *reasons* possibly a pun on "raisins" (see p. 167).

PRINCE

I'll be no longer guilty of this sin. This sanguine coward, this
bed-presser, this horseback-breaker, this huge hill of flesh . . .

FALSTAFF

210   'Sblood, you starveling, you eel-skin, you dried neat's-tongue,
you bull's-pizzle, you stock-fish!—O for breath to utter what
is like thee—you tailor's yard, you sheath, you bow-case, you
vile standing tuck! . . .

PRINCE

Well, breathe awhile, and then to it again; and when thou hast
215   tired thyself in base comparisons hear me speak but this.

POINS

Mark, Jack.

PRINCE

We two saw you four set on four, and bound them and were
masters of their wealth. Mark now how a plain tale shall put
you down—then did we two set on you four, and with a word
220   outfaced you from your prize, and have it, yea and can show it
you here in the house: and, Falstaff, you carried your guts

---

208. *sanguine*   one of the four types of personality and physique
produced by the humors or bodily secretions, according to early medical theory; they were sanguine (full-blooded), choleric (compare Hotspur), melancholic (Hamlet), and phlegmatic (Northumberland?).
Cowards were not usually sanguine.

210. *eel*   QqF have variants of "elf-skin"; but "eel-skin" is easily
so misread, alludes pointedly to Hal's slim physique (compare II.ii.55,
and note), and is used again by Falstaff (in *2HIV*, III.ii.325) in ridicul-
ing the "starved justice," Shallow.

211. *pizzle*   Apparently, the dried penis of a bull was used for
flogging; Hal is thus identified here with a particularly unpleasant kind
of whip. *stock-fish*   dry salted cod.

212. *bow-case*   a leather case to hold bows not strung taut for use.

213. *standing tuck*   an unpliant ("standing" was a technical term)
rapier—with a pun on "standing."

217. *set . . . bound*   Such a change of mood often occurs in Elizabethan English.

219. *with*   probably meaning "by" rather than "in."

away as nimbly, with as quick dexterity, and roared for mercy, and still run and roared, as ever I heard bull-calf. What a slave art thou to hack thy sword as thou hast done, and then say it
225   was in fight! What trick, what device, what starting-hole canst thou now find out, to hide thee from this open and apparent shame?

POINS

Come, let's hear, Jack—what trick hast thou now?

FALSTAFF

By the Lord, I knew ye as well as he that made ye. Why, hear
230   you, my masters—was it for me to kill the heir-apparent? Should I turn upon the true prince? Why, thou knowest I am as valiant as Hercules; but beware instinct—the lion will not touch the true prince; instinct is a great matter. I was now a coward on instinct; I shall think the better of myself, and thee,
235   during my life—I for a valiant lion, and thou for a true prince. But by the Lord, lads, I am glad you have the money. Hostess, clap to the doors!—watch tonight, pray tomorrow. Gallants, lads, boys, hearts of gold—all the titles of good fellowship come to you! What shall we be merry, shall we have a play
240   extempore?

PRINCE

Content, and the argument shall be thy running away.

FALSTAFF

Ah, no more of that, Hal, and thou lovest me.

---

225. *starting-hole*   a hole to which a mouse "starts," or darts, for refuge; here it means "subterfuge," by which to conceal cowardice.

226. *apparent*   obvious.

232–3. *lion . . . prince*   an ancient belief; Humphreys quotes the life of Hastings (lines 282–3) in *Mirror for Magistrates*: "Lions . . . fear the sacred laws/ Of princes' blood."

237. *watch . . . tomorrow*   stay awake tonight (to drink), repent tomorrow (with a hangover?)—a play on Matthew 26:41, "Watch and pray, that ye enter not into temptation."

Enter Hostess.

HOSTESS

O Jesu, my lord the Prince!

PRINCE

How now, my lady the hostess!—what sayest thou to me?

HOSTESS

245 Marry, my lord, there is a nobleman of the court at door would speak with you: he says he comes from your father.

PRINCE

Give him as much as will make him a royal man, and send him back again to my mother.

FALSTAFF

What manner of man is he?

HOSTESS

250 An old man.

FALSTAFF

What doth Gravity out of his bed at midnight? Shall I give him his answer?

PRINCE

Prithee do, Jack.

FALSTAFF

Faith, and I'll send him packing.

Exit.

PRINCE

255 Now sirs, by'r Lady, you fought fair, so did you Peto, so did you Bardolph; you are lions too, you ran away upon instinct, you will not touch the true prince, no—fie!

BARDOLPH

Faith, I ran when I saw others run.

PRINCE

Faith, tell me now in earnest, how came Falstaff's sword so
260 hacked?

245–7. *nobleman . . . royal man*   a pun on the names of coins. A noble was worth a third of a pound; a royal, half a pound.

PETO

Why, he hacked it with his dagger, and said he would swear
Truth out of England, but he would make you believe it was
done in fight, and persuaded us to do the like.

BARDOLPH

Yea, and to tickle our noses with spear-grass, to make them
265 bleed, and then to beslubber our garments with it, and swear it
was the blood of true men. I did that I did not this seven year
before, I blushed to hear his monstrous devices.

PRINCE

O villain, thou stolest a cup of sack eighteen years ago and
wert taken with the manner, and ever since thou hast blushed
270 extempore. Thou hadst fire and sword on thy side, and yet
thou ran'st away; what instinct hadst thou for it?

BARDOLPH [*pointing to his face*]

My lord, do you see these meteors? Do you behold these exhalations?

PRINCE

I do.

BARDOLPH

275 What think you they portend?

261–2. *swear . . . England*   swear so much that Truth would not be
able to stay in England to face him.

264. *spear-grass*   spearwort, a poisonous plant with sharply
pointed leaves.

265. *beslubber*   daub. This is a trick taken from the behavior of a
coward, Derick, in *The Famous Victories*, who feigned wounds to avoid
being sent into battle: "I would take a straw and thrust it into my nose,
and make my nose bleed."

269. *taken with the manner*   caught with the thing stolen (a legal
term, from French *manoeuvre*: "handwork," later meaning the thing
handled). A pun on the more modern sense may be intended: attracted
by the custom.

270. *fire*   his red face.

272–3. *exhalations*   any meteor or comet; they were taken as "portents" or evil omens.

PRINCE

Hot livers, and cold purses.

BARDOLPH

Choler, my lord, if rightly taken.

PRINCE

No, if rightly taken, halter.

[*Re-*]*enter* FALSTAFF.

Here comes lean Jack, here comes bare bone. How now, my
280   sweet creature of bombast, how long is't ago, Jack, since thou
sawest thine own knee?

FALSTAFF

My own knee! When I was about thy years, Hal, I was not
an eagle's talon in the waist—I could have crept into any
alderman's thumb-ring: a plague of sighing and grief, it blows
285   a man up like a bladder. There's villainous news abroad; here
was Sir John Bracy from your father: you must to the court in
the morning. That same mad fellow of the North, Percy, and
he of Wales that gave Amamon the bastinado, and made Lucifer cuckold, and swore the devil his true liegeman upon the
290   cross of a Welsh hook—what a plague call you him?

---

276. *hot livers* Charmian, in *A&C*, I.ii.23, says "I had rather heat
my liver with drinking."

277. *choler* either a fiery (and easily provoked) temperament, or
anger (at the jests).

278. *halter* the hangman's noose, a pun on *choler* and *collar* (*taken*
meant both "understood" and "arrested").

280. *bombast* cotton stuffing used to pad clothing.

283. *talon* talent QqF.

284. *thumb-ring* a heavy ring used as a seal by substantial citizens.

288. *Amamon* a devil. *bastinado* beating on the soles of the feet.

288-9. *made Lucifer cuckold* gave the Devil his horns. The morning star, often called Lucifer (*lux*, light; *ferre*, to bear), was identified
with Satan as leader of the fallen angels; the symbol of cuckoldry was
a pair of horns.

290. *Welsh hook* a pike with a hook, resembling the instruments
of torture given to devils in medieval paintings of Hell—more suitable

POINS

O—Glendower.

FALSTAFF

Owen, Owen—the same; and his son-in-law, Mortimer, and old Northumberland, and that sprightly Scot of Scots, Douglas, that runs a-horseback up a hill perpendicular . . .

PRINCE

295   He that rides at high speed, and with his pistol kills a sparrow flying.

FALSTAFF

You have hit it.

PRINCE

So did he never the sparrow.

FALSTAFF

Well, that rascal hath good mettle in him—he will not run.

PRINCE

300   Why, what a rascal art thou then, to praise him so for running!

FALSTAFF

A-horseback, ye cuckoo, but afoot he will not budge a foot.

PRINCE

Yes, Jack, upon instinct.

FALSTAFF

I grant ye, upon instinct. Well, he is there too, and one Murdoch, and a thousand blue-caps more. Worcester is stolen away

---

for diabolic oaths of allegiance than the cross of a sword, as it had little resemblance to a cross.

299. *mettle*   mettall Q1, explaining the pun: Falstaff praises Douglas for his "mettle" (courage), but also he implies that good "metal" does not run (i.e., melt easily), though Douglas does run according to Falstaff, as Hal points out; the passage bears on Douglas' behavior in the battle later, V.v.17*ff.*

301. *cuckoo*   here considered to resemble the parrot in its senseless repetition.

304. *caps*   Scots bonnets (with their wearers).

305   tonight; thy father's beard is turned white with the news; you may buy land now as cheap as stinking mackerel.

PRINCE

Why then, it is like, if there come a hot June and this civil buffeting hold, we shall buy maidenheads as they buy hobnails, by the hundreds.

FALSTAFF

310   By the mass, lad, thou sayest true—it is like we shall have good trading that way. But tell me, Hal, art not thou horrible afeard? Thou being heir-apparent, could the world pick thee out three such enemies again as that fiend Douglas, that spirit Percy, and that devil Glendower? Art thou not horribly afraid?
315   Doth not thy blood thrill at it?

PRINCE

Not a whit, i'faith—I lack some of thy instinct.

FALSTAFF

Well, thou wilt be horribly chid tomorrow when thou comest to thy father; if thou love me, practise an answer.

PRINCE

Do thou stand for my father and examine me upon the particu-
320   lars of my life.

FALSTAFF

Shall I? Content! This chair shall be my state, this dagger my sceptre, and this cushion my crown.

PRINCE

Thy state is taken for a joint-stool, thy golden sceptre for a leaden dagger, and thy precious rich crown for a pitiful bald
325   crown.

308–9. *we . . . hundreds*   because of the inevitable assaults the women expected from the soldiers.

313. *spirit*   in the sense of mischievous spirit, to match "fiend" and "devil."

321. *state*   throne.

323. *joint-stool*   a stool with properly made joints.

324. *leaden dagger*   a typical stage prop.

FALSTAFF

Well, and the fire of grace be not quite out of thee, now shalt thou be moved. Give me a cup of sack to make my eyes look red, that it may be thought that I have wept, for I must speak in passion, and I will do it in King Cambyses' vein.

PRINCE

330   Well, here is my leg.

FALSTAFF

And here is my speech. Stand aside, nobility.

HOSTESS

O Jesu, this is excellent sport, i'faith.

FALSTAFF

Weep not sweet queen, for trickling tears are vain.

HOSTESS

O the Father, how he holds his countenance!

FALSTAFF

335   For God's sake, lords, convey my tristful queen,
For tears do stop the flood-gates of her eyes.

HOSTESS

O Jesu, he doth it as like one of these harlotry players as ever I see!

FALSTAFF

Peace, good pint-pot, peace good tickle-brain.—Harry, I do
340   not only marvel where thou spendest thy time, but also how

---

329. *King Cambyses' vein*   T. Preston's tragedy, *Cambyses, King of Persia* (1570) was full of rhetoric a little like Hotspur's, or the King's. "Weep not sweet Queen . . ." (line 333) is a fair example, even faintly echoing lines in Preston's play, and others like it.

330. *leg*   a deep bow with one leg bent, the other drawn back.

335. *convey*   escort. *tristful*   sad. QqF read "trustful," emended by Rowe (whose generally accepted reading appears in the early 17th-century Dering ms. of the play also. The ms. has no certain authority).

337. *harlotry*   rascal (used playfully here).

339. *tickle-brain*   Falstaff's names for the hostess allude to her liquor and its effects.

thou art accompanied. For though the camomile, the more it is
trodden on, the faster it grows, yet youth, the more it is wasted
the sooner it wears. That thou art my son I have partly thy
mother's word, partly my own opinion, but chiefly a villainous
345 trick of thine eye, and a foolish hanging of thy nether lip, that
doth warrant me. If then thou be son to me, here lies the point
—why, being son to me, art thou so pointed at? Shall the
blessed sun of heaven prove a micher, and eat blackberries?—
a question not to be asked. Shall the son of England prove a
350 thief, and take purses?—a question to be asked. There is a
thing, Harry, which thou hast often heard of, and it is known
to many in our land by the name of pitch. This pitch, as ancient writers do report, doth defile; so doth the company thou
keepest. For, Harry, now I do not speak to thee in drink, but
355 in tears; not in pleasure, but in passion; not in words only,
but in woes also: and yet there is a virtuous man whom I have
often noted in thy company, but I know not his name.

PRINCE

What manner of man, and it like your majesty?

FALSTAFF

A goodly portly man, i'faith, and a corpulent, of a cheerful
360 look, a pleasing eye, and a most noble carriage, and, as I think,
his age some fifty, or, by'r Lady, inclining to threescore; and
now I remember me, his name is Falstaff. If that man should

341–3. *camomile ... wears* Kittredge notes the echo of Lyly in his
elaborately rhetorical *Euphues* (1578): "Though the Camomile, the
more it is trodden and pressed down, the more it spreadeth, yet the
violet the oftner it is handled and touched, the sooner it withereth and
decayeth" (Bond, I,196). The "yet" here, as in Qq3–5,F, justifies that
in the text, where Qq1–2 awkwardly read "so." Camomile is an aro-
matic herb.

348. *sun* like the lion, a symbol of kingship. *prove a micher* play
truant, skulk (compare *mooch*); blackberries are a familiar attraction
for truants.

353. *writers* Ecclesiasticus 8:1—quoted in *Euphues* (Bond, I,205).

359. *portly* dignified. *corpulent* well built (not "fat," as now).

be lewdly given, he deceiveth me, for, Harry, I see virtue in his
looks. If then the tree may be known by the fruit, as the fruit
365 by the tree, then peremptorily I speak it—there is virtue in
that Falstaff; him keep with, the rest banish. And tell me now,
thou naughty varlet, tell me where hast thou been this month?

PRINCE

Dost you speak like a king?—do thou stand for me and I'll
play my father.

FALSTAFF

370 Depose me?—if thou dost it half so gravely, so majestically,
both in word and matter, hang me up by the heels for a rabbit-
sucker, or a poulter's hare.

PRINCE

Well, here I am set.

FALSTAFF

And here I stand—judge, my masters!

PRINCE

375 Now, Harry, whence come you?

FALSTAFF

My noble lord, from Eastcheap.

PRINCE

The complaints I hear of thee are grievous.

FALSTAFF

'Sblood, my lord, they are false.—Nay, I'll tickle ye for a
young prince, i'faith.

PRINCE

380 Swearest thou, ungracious boy?—henceforth ne'er look on me!
Thou art violently carried away from grace, there is a devil

---

363. *lewdly given* basely inclined; "lewd" originally meant ignorant, and thence, base or wicked.

364–5. *tree . . . tree* See Matthew 8:33: "The tree is known by the
fruit," also quoted in *Euphues* (Bond, I,207).

367. *varlet* boy (an everyday word, out of place in the speech).

371–2. *rabbit-sucker* baby rabbit. *poulter* poulterer.

378. *tickle ye for* make you spectators laugh by acting as.

haunts thee in the likeness of an old fat man, a tun of man is thy companion. Why dost thou converse with that trunk of humours, that bolting-hutch of beastliness, that swollen parcel
385 of dropsies, that huge bombard of sack, that stuffed cloak-bag of guts, that roasted Manningtree ox with the pudding in his belly, that reverend Vice, that grey Iniquity, that father Ruffian, that Vanity in years? Wherein is he good, but to taste sack and drink it? wherein neat and cleanly, but to carve a capon
390 and eat it? wherein cunning, but in craft? wherein crafty, but in villainy? wherein villainous, but in all things? wherein worthy, but in nothing?

FALSTAFF

I would your grace would take me with you—whom means your grace?

PRINCE

395 That villainous, abominable misleader of youth, Falstaff, that old white-bearded Satan.

FALSTAFF

My lord, the man I know.

PRINCE

I know thou dost.

FALSTAFF

But to say I know more harm in him than in myself, were to

---

384. *humours* potentially unhealthy secretions (see note at line 208). *bolting-hutch* a large bin for sifting flour.

385. *bombard* a large leather wine sack. Compare *Temp*, II.ii.20: "Yond same black cloud, yond huge one, looks like a foul bombard that would shed his liquor."

386. *Manningtree* a town in Essex; whether famous for cattle or not, it was the scene of morality play performances with characters like those next mentioned by Hal—Vice, Iniquity, Ruffian (possibly a name for the Devil; see *OED: ruffin*), Vanity. *pudding* like puddings in Scotland today, Elizabethan ones consisted of meat and herbs stuffed into animal intestines.

390. *cunning* skillful.

393. *take me with you* help me to follow your thought.

400   say more than I know. That he is old, the more the pity, his
white hairs do witness it; but that he is, saving your reverence,
a whoremaster, that I utterly deny. If sack and sugar be a fault,
God help the wicked! If to be old and merry be a sin, then
many an old host that I know is damned. If to be fat be to be
405   hated, then Pharoah's lean kine are to be loved. No, my good
lord—banish Peto, banish Bardolph, banish Poins, but for
sweet Jack Falstaff, kind Jack Falstaff, true Jack Falstaff, valiant Jack Falstaff, and therefore more valiant being as he is old
Jack Falstaff, banish not him thy Harry's company, banish not
410   him thy Harry's company: banish plump Jack, and banish all
the world.

PRINCE

I do, I will.

[Knocking and cries offstage. Hostess, FRANCIS, and
BARDOLPH leave.]

[Re-]enter BARDOLPH, running.

BARDOLPH

O my lord, my lord—the sheriff with a most monstrous watch
is at the door.

FALSTAFF

415   Out, ye rogue—play out the play; I have much to say in behalf
of that Falstaff.

[Re-]enter the Hostess.

HOSTESS

O Jesu, my lord, my lord!

---

401. *saving your reverence* without meaning to offend you.

405. *lean kine* in Genesis 41 these brought famine.

412. *S.D.* QqF do not note the departure of Bardolph and the hostess, only their return; the knocking seems the most likely reason for
their departure. *most . . . watch* very large posse.

418. *Heigh . . . stick* This is the Devil's own dance. Kittredge notes
that dance music was associated with the Devil; F. Beaumont's and J.
Fletcher's *Humorous Lieutenant*, IV.4 (Glover and Waller, II,349):
"such a jig! for certain, gentlemen,/ The Fiend rides on a fiddlestick."

PRINCE

Heigh, heigh, the devil rides upon a fiddle-stick. What's the matter?

HOSTESS

420 The sheriff and all the watch are at the door; they are come to search the house. Shall I let them in?

FALSTAFF

Dost thou hear, Hal? Never call a true piece of gold a counter-feit: thou art essentially made, without seeming so.

PRINCE

And thou a natural coward without instinct.

FALSTAFF

425 I deny your major—if you will deny the sheriff, so; if not, let him enter. If I become not a cart as well as another man, a plague on my bringing up! I hope I shall as soon be strangled with a halter as another.

PRINCE

Go hide thee behind the arras, the rest walk up above. Now,
430 my masters, for a true face, and good conscience.

FALSTAFF

Both which I have had, but their date is out, and therefore I'll hide me.

[FALSTAFF *hides; all but the* PRINCE *and* PETO *leave.*]

---

423. *thou . . . so*   You (for example) have substantial worth despite your low appearance. It seems Falstaff is still preoccupied with Hal's denunciation, lines 381*ff*. Many editors, feeling this is unlikely, alter the text awkwardly (e.g., reading "mad" for "made"). "Essence" and "substance" are scholastic terms for the basic reality of things.

425. *major*   major premise; another suggestion of scholastic de-bate, not necessarily an exact one, but allowing a pun—major (*maior* Q1) is pronounced "mayor" and balanced with the other municipal of-ficial, "sheriff."

426. *become a cart*   adorn the cart carrying me to the gallows.

429. *arras*   Walls were decorated by tapestries (often made at Arras in northern France) hung on projecting frames. The curtained inner stage is used here.

PRINCE

Call in the sheriff.

Enter Sheriff *and the* Carrier.

Now, Master Sheriff, what is your will with me?

SHERIFF

435   First pardon me, my lord. A hue and cry
Hath followed certain men unto this house.

PRINCE

What men?

SHERIFF

One of them is well known, my gracious lord,
A gross fat man.

CARRIER

As fat as butter.

PRINCE

440   The man, I do assure you, is not here,
For I myself at this time have employed him,
And, sheriff, I will engage my word to thee
That I will by tomorrow dinner-time
Send him to answer thee, or any man,
445   For anything he shall be charged withal;
And so let me entreat you leave the house.

SHERIFF

I will, my lord. There are two gentlemen
Have in this robbery lost three hundred marks.

PRINCE

It may be so; if he have robbed these men
450   He shall be answerable, and so farewell.

---

435. *hue and cry*   All citizens hearing the shout of those pursuing
a criminal were supposed to join the pursuit; a kind of spontaneous
posse.
440. *not here*   not just here—an equivocation.
445. *withal*   with (used at the end of a period).

SHERIFF

Good night, my noble lord.

PRINCE

I think it is good morrow, is it not?

SHERIFF

Indeed, my lord, I think it be two o'clock.

Exit [with Carrier].

PRINCE

This oily rascal is known as well as Paul's; go call him forth.

PETO

455   Falstaff!—Fast asleep behind the arras, and snorting like a horse.

PRINCE

Hark how hard he fetches breath—search his pockets. ([PETO] *searcheth* [FALSTAFF'S] *pockets, and findeth certain papers.*) What hast thou found?

PETO

Nothing but papers, my lord.

PRINCE

460   Let's see what they be, read them.

[PETO *reads*]

Item: a capon	2s. 2d.
Item: sauce	4d.
Item: sack, two gallons	5s. 8d.
Item: anchovies, and sack	
465 after supper	2s. 6d.
Item: bread	ob.

---

454. *Paul's*   St. Paul's cathedral.

461. PETO   Qq neglect to give the reading of the account to Peto, though the Prince's "read them" is clear enough.

464. *anchovies*   as now, appetizers and thirst provokers.

466. *ob*   obolus (a small Greek coin), used as the Latin name for halfpenny (compare Latin *denarius*—a penny—written "d." in Falstaff's bill).

[PRINCE]

O, monstrous! But one halfpennyworth of bread to this intol-
erable deal of sack! What there is else keep close, we'll read it
at more advantage. There let him sleep till day; I'll to the court
470 in the morning. We must all to the wars, and [*to* FALSTAFF]
thy place shall be honorable!—I'll procure this fat rogue a
charge of foot, and I know his death will be a march of twelve
score. The money shall be paid back again with advantage. Be
with me betimes in the morning; and so good morrow, Peto.

PETO

475 Good morrow, my lord.

Exeunt.

[*Act III, scene i: At the Archdeacon of Bangor's house, in
Wales, some time later than II.iii.*] *Enter* HOTSPUR, WORCESTER,
LORD MORTIMER, OWEN GLENDOWER.

MORTIMER

Those promises are fair, the parties sure,
And our induction full of prosperous hope.

---

469. *at more advantage*   at a more advantageous time.

471. *thy place*   For some reason, editors address this to Peto, while
feeling it is inappropriate (even switching Poins for him as the one who
stays with the Prince because of it). Clearly, Hal is apostrophizing the
sleeping Falstaff, explaining himself immediately afterward to Peto.

472. *charge of foot*   command of a company of infantry.

472–3. *twelve score*   yards. *advantage*   addition.

S.D.   The only clue to the setting of this scene lies in Holinshed's ob-
servation (1807, III,24) that the rebels' agreement was made "by their
deputies, in the house of the archdeacon of Bangor" (see line 69). This
setting was first suggested by Theobald. *NCS* suggests "Glendower's
house."

2. *induction*   opening scene, preceding the main action, as in
Shrew.

HOTSPUR

Lord Mortimer, and cousin Glendower
Will you sit down? and uncle Worcester.
5   A plague upon it!—I have forgot the map.

GLENDOWER

No, here it is. Sit, cousin Percy,
Sit, good cousin Hotspur—for by that name
As oft as Lancaster doth speak of you,
His cheek looks pale, and with a rising sigh
He wisheth you in heaven.

HOTSPUR

10   And you in hell,
As oft as he hears Owen Glendower spoke of.

GLENDOWER

I cannot blame him: at my nativity
The front of heaven was full of fiery shapes
Of burning cressets, and at my birth
15   The frame and huge foundations of the earth
Shaked like a coward.

HOTSPUR

                   Why so it would have done
At the same season if your mother's cat
Had but kittened—though yourself had never been born.

GLENDOWER

I say the earth did shake when I was born.

HOTSPUR

20   And I say the earth was not of my mind,
If you suppose as fearing you it shook.

3–9. These lines are prose in Qq, perhaps because of a compositor's
mistake in reading the manuscript.

8. *Lancaster*   The king was Duke of Lancaster.

13. *front*   forehead (Latin *frons*).

14. *cressets*   a light carried in a metal basket, suspended from a
pole.

GLENDOWER

The heavens were all on fire, the earth did tremble . . .

HOTSPUR

O, then the earth shook to see the heavens on fire,
And not in fear of your nativity.
25 Diseasèd nature oftentimes breaks forth
In strange eruptions, oft the teeming earth
Is with a kind of colic pinched and vexed
By the imprisoning of unruly wind
Within her womb, which for enlargement striving
30 Shakes the old beldam earth, and topples down
Steeples and moss-grown towers. At your birth
Our grandam earth, having this distemp'rature,
In passion shook.

GLENDOWER

Cousin, of many men
I do not bear these crossings . . . give me leave
35 To tell you once again that at my birth
The front of heaven was full of fiery shapes,
The goats ran from the mountains, and the herds
Were strangely clamorous to the frighted fields.
These signs have marked me extraordinary,
40 And all the courses of my life do show
I am not in the roll of common men:

    25–33. *Diseasèd . . . shook* Compare Gabriel Harvey's *Pleasant . . . Discourse of the Earthquake,* 1580 (Grosart, I,52): "The material cause of earthquakes (as . . . is sufficiently proved by Aristotle in the second book of his *Meteors*) is no doubt great abundance of wind . . . emprisoned in the caves, and dungeons of the earth: which wind or vapours, seeking to be set at liberty . . . violently rush out, and as it were break prison, which forcible eruption, and strong breath, causeth an earthquake."
    30. *beldam* grandmother; compare line 32.
    32. *distemp'rature* disorder.
    33. *passion* suffering (from Latin *pati,* to suffer).
    34. *crossings* contradictions.

Where is he living, clipped in with the sea
That chides the banks of England, Scotland, Wales,
Which calls me pupil or hath read to me?
45 And bring him out that is but woman's son
Can trace me in the tedious ways of Art,
And hold me pace in deep experiments.

HOTSPUR

I think there's no man speaks better Welsh;
I'll to dinner!

MORTIMER

50 Peace, cousin Percy, you will make him mad.

GLENDOWER

I can call spirits from the vasty deep.

HOTSPUR

Why so can I, or so can any man,
But will they come when you do call for them?

GLENDOWER

Why, I can teach you, cousin, to command the Devil.

HOTSPUR

55 And I can teach thee, coz, to shame the Devil—
By telling truth. Tell truth and shame the Devil:
If thou have power to raise him bring him hither,
And I'll be sworn I have power to shame him hence.
O, while you live, tell truth and shame the Devil!

---

42. *clipped in with*   embraced by.

43. *chides*   used metaphorically for the physical movement of the sea against the land.

44. *read to*   taught (compare "readers" in English universities).

46. *trace*   follow. *tedious*   laborious. *Art*   magic.

47. *hold me pace*   keep pace with me.

48. *Welsh*   Most editors feel that Hotspur uses the word satirically, to mean barbarous jargon.

51. *vasty deep*   the bottom of Hell.

54. This is an irregularly long line, probably shortened by elisions in delivery.

56. *Tell . . . Devil*   a proverb.

MORTIMER

60 Come, come, no more of this unprofitable chat.

GLENDOWER

Three times hath Henry Bolingbroke made head
Against my power, thrice from the banks of Wye
And sandy-bottomed Severn have I sent him
Bootless home, and weather-beaten back.

HOTSPUR

65 Home without boots, and in foul weather too!
How 'scapes he agues in the Devil's name?

GLENDOWER

Come, here is the map; shall we divide our right
According to our threefold order ta'en?

MORTIMER

The archdeacon hath divided it
70 Into three limits very equally:
England from Trent and Severn hitherto,
By south and east is to my part assigned;
All westward, Wales beyond the Severn shore,
And all the fertile land within that bound
75 To Owen Glendower; and, dear coz, to you
The remnant northward lying off from Trent.
And our indentures tripartite are drawn,
Which being sealèd interchangeably

---

61. *Three times* The third time (1405) actually postdated the
Percys' revolt (1402). *made head* mustered an army.

64. *bootless* without profit. *weather-beaten* Holinshed (1807, III,
20): "through art magic, [Glendower] caused such foul weather . . .
that the king was constrained to return home."

66. *agues* fevers.

67. *our right* the land we rightfully claim.

68. *order* arrangement.

70. *limits* territories with specified boundaries.

71. *hitherto* as far as this point.

77. *indentures tripartite* contracts in triplicate.

78. *sealèd interchangeably* Each of the three would possess a copy
similarly stamped with the seals of the contracting parties.

(A business that this night may execute)

80 Tomorrow, cousin Percy, you and I
And my good Lord of Worcester will set forth
To meet your father and the Scottish power,
As is appointed us, at Shrewsbury.
My father Glendower is not ready yet,

85 Nor shall we need his help these fourteen days.
[*To* GLEN.] Within that space you may have drawn together
Your tenants, friends, and neighbouring gentlemen.

GLENDOWER

A shorter time shall send me to you, lords,
And in my conduct shall your ladies come,

90 From whom you now must steal and take no leave,
For there will be a world of water shed
Upon the parting of your wives and you.

HOTSPUR

Methinks my moiety, north from Burton here,
In quantity equals not one of yours:

95 See how this river comes me cranking in,
And cuts me from the best of all my land,
A huge half-moon, a monstrous cantle out.
I'll have the current in this place dammed up,
And here the smug and silver Trent shall run

100 In a new channel fair and evenly;
It shall not wind with such a deep indent,
To rob me of so rich a bottom here.

GLENDOWER

Not wind? It shall, it must—you see it doth.

---

84. *father*   father-in-law.
93. *moiety*   share (obviously not meaning "half" here).
95. *comes me cranking in*   winds into my territory.
97. *cantle*   scantle QqF—but this means "trifle" (compare *scant*); *cantle* (corner, slice) makes the necessary sense—the "s" may have carried from "monstrous." Hotspur's corrective plan is implausible.
99. *smug*   neat; hence, here, "smooth."
102. *bottom*   low-lying land.

MORTIMER

Yea, but—
105 Mark how he bears his course, and runs me up
With like advantage on the other side,
Gelding the opposèd continent as much
As on the other side it takes from you.

WORCESTER

Yea, but a little charge will trench him here,
110 And on this north side win this cape of land,
And then he runs straight and even.

HOTSPUR

I'll have it so; a little charge will do it.

GLENDOWER

I'll not have it altered.

HOTSPUR

                    Will not you?

GLENDOWER

No, nor you shall not.

HOTSPUR

                    Who shall say me nay?

GLENDOWER

Why, that will I.

HOTSPUR

115   Let me not understand you then:
Speak it in Welsh!

GLENDOWER

I can speak English, lord, as well as you,
For I was trained up in the English court,
Where being but young I framed to the harp

104–8. Prose in Qq, but all editors agree the passage is verse. The
short line may mark a pause while Mortimer checks the map.

107. *Gelding* suggesting the fertility of the region. *continent* that
which contains; here, a boundary or river bank.

109. *charge* expense.

120   Many an English ditty lovely well,
        And gave the tongue a helpful ornament,
        A virtue that was never seen in you.

                        HOTSPUR
        Marry,
        And I am glad of it with all my heart!
125   I had rather be a kitten and cry "mew,"
        Than one of these same metre ballad-mongers;
        I had rather hear a brazen canstick turned,
        Or a dry wheel grate on the axle-tree,
        And that would set my teeth nothing on edge,
130   Nothing so much as mincing poetry—
        'Tis like the forced gait of a shuffling nag.

                        GLENDOWER
        Come, you shall have Trent turned.

                        HOTSPUR
        I do not care—I'll give thrice so much land
        To any well-deserving friend;
135   But in the way of bargain, mark ye me,
        I'll cavil on the ninth part of a hair.
        Are the indentures drawn? shall we be gone?

                        GLENDOWER
        The moon shines fair—you may away by night:
        I'll haste the writer, and withal
140   Break with your wives of your departure hence.
        I am afraid my daughter will run mad,
        So much she doteth on her Mortimer.

                                            Exit.

---

        121. *helpful ornament*   with his musical setting.
        126. *metre*   the association with ballads (see II.ii.37) suggests that
"doggerel" is meant here.
        127. *canstick*   candlestick. *turned*   on a lathe, for shaping or pol-
ishing (an almost proverbially noisy process).
        130. *mincing*   mannered.
        131. *forced . . . nag*   the constrained movement of a hobbled horse.
        140. *Break with*   inform.

MORTIMER

Fie, cousin Percy, how you cross my father!

HOTSPUR

I cannot choose; sometimes he angers me
145   With telling me of the moldwarp and the ant,
Of the dreamer Merlin and his prophecies,
And of a dragon and a finless fish,
A clip-winged griffin and a moulten raven,
A couching lion and a ramping cat,
150   And such a deal of skimble-skamble stuff
As puts me from my faith. I tell you what—
He held me last night at least nine hours
In reckoning up the several devils' names
That were his lackeys. I cried "Hum," and "Well, go to,"
155   But mark'd him not a word. O, he is as tedious
As a tired horse, a railing wife,
Worse than a smoky house. I had rather live
With cheese and garlic in a windmill, far,
Than feed on cates and have him talk to me,
160   In any summer house in Christendom.

MORTIMER

In faith, he is a worthy gentleman,

---

144. *choose*   to do otherwise.

145. *moldwarp*   mole. Compare Holinshed (1807, III,24): "a vain prophecy, as though King Henry was the moldwarp, cursed of God's own mouth, and they three were the dragon, the lion, and the wolf."

146. *Merlin*   the Welsh magician at King Arthur's court.

149. *ramping*   rearing fiercely (of heraldic animals, usually).

150. *skimble-skamble*   nonsensical (*OED* says the word appears no earlier than in this passage—Shakespeare may have invented the term for Hotspur).

151. *puts . . . faith*   makes me skeptical even of my religion.

153. *several*   various.

154. *go to*   indeed! or some such polite expression of surprise.

155–7. *as tedious . . . house*   traditional comparisons; compare Proverbs 10:26 and 21:19.

159. *cates*   delicacies.

160. *summer house*   country house.

Exceedingly well read, and profited
In strange concealments, valiant as a lion,
And wondrous affable, and as bountiful
165 As mines of India. Shall I tell you, cousin?—
He holds your temper in a high respect
And curbs himself even of his natural scope
When you come 'cross his humour, faith he does!
I warrant you that man is not alive
170 Might so have tempted him as you have done,
Without the taste of danger and reproof—
But do not use it oft, let me entreat you.

WORCESTER

In faith, my lord, you are too wilful-blame,
And since your coming hither have done enough
175 To put him quite besides his patience.
You must needs learn, lord, to amend this fault—
Though sometimes it show greatness, courage, blood,
(And that's the dearest grace it renders you)
Yet oftentimes it doth present harsh rage,
180 Defect of manners, want of government,
Pride, haughtiness, opinion, and disdain,
The least of which haunting a nobleman
Loseth men's hearts and leaves behind a stain
Upon the beauty of all parts besides,
185 Beguiling them of commendation.

162–3. *profited . . . concealments*   skilled in obscure arts.
173. *wilful-blame*   blameworthy for your wilfulness. The *OED* notes "the dative infinitive *to blame* is much used as the predicate after *be.* In the 16–17th c. the *to* was misunderstood as *too,* and blame taken as adj."
177. *blood*   spirit.
178. *dearest grace*   highest excellence.
180. *government*   self-control.
181. *opinion*   self-esteem (in the sense of "opinionated").
184. *parts*   abilities (compare "a man of parts").
185. *Beguiling them*   tricking them out of.

HOTSPUR

Well, I am schooled—good manners be your speed!
Here come our wives, and let us take our leave.

Enter GLENDOWER *with the* Ladies.

MORTIMER

This is the deadly spite that angers me,
My wife can speak no English, I no Welsh.

GLENDOWER

190   My daughter weeps; she'll not part with you,
She'll be a soldier too, she'll to the wars.

MORTIMER

Good father, tell her that she and my Aunt Percy
Shall follow in your conduct speedily.

      GLENDOWER *speaks to her in Welsh,*
      and she answers him in the same.

GLENDOWER

She is desperate here, a peevish, self-willed harlotry, one that
195   no persuasion can do good upon.

The lady speaks in Welsh.

MORTIMER

I understand thy looks—that pretty Welsh
Which thou pourest down from these swelling heavens,

---

186. *be your speed*   help you on your way.

192. *Aunt*   The two Mortimers are again confused—Lady Percy
was the sister of the Mortimer who married Glendower's daughter
(compare line 84), aunt to the other Mortimer.

193. *conduct*   escort.

194. *desperate here*   if she stays without her husband. *harlotry*
wench (in a playful sense).

196. *that pretty Welsh*   the "language" of her tears.

197. *these swelling heavens*   her tear-swollen eyes (it was a Petrar-
chan conceit to call one's mistress' eyes "heavenly," because of the effect of her glance on the lover).

I am too perfect in, and but for shame
In such a parley should I answer thee.

The lady [speaks] again in Welsh.

MORTIMER

200   I understand thy kisses, and thou mine,
And that's a feeling disputation;
But I will never be a truant, love,
Till I have learnt thy language, for thy tongue
Makes Welsh as sweet as ditties highly penned,
205   Sung by a fair queen in a summer's bower
With ravishing division, to her lute.

GLENDOWER

Nay, if you melt, then will she run mad.

The lady speaks again in Welsh.

MORTIMER

O, I am ignorance itself in this.

GLENDOWER

She bids you on the wanton rushes lay you down,
210   And rest your gentle head upon her lap,
And she will sing the song that pleaseth you,
And on your eyelids crown the god of sleep,
Charming your blood with pleasing heaviness,
Making such difference 'twixt wake and sleep
215   As is the difference betwixt day and night,
The hour before the heavenly-harnessed team
Begins his golden progress in the east.

---

199. *In such . . . thee*   I should weep in reply.
201. *feeling disputation*   deep-felt exchange.
206. *division*   an ornamented restatement of a simple melody, usually breaking long notes into several quicker ones.
207. *melt*   lose your composure.
209. *wanton*   lush and comfortable.
212. *crown the god of sleep*   give sleep authority.
216. *heavenly . . . team*   the chariot of the sungod, Phoebus.

MORTIMER

With all my heart I'll sit and hear her sing;
By that time will our book, I think, be drawn.

GLENDOWER

220 Do so, and those musicians that shall play to you,
Hang in the air a thousand leagues from hence,
And straight they shall be here; sit and attend.

HOTSPUR

Come, Kate, thou art perfect in lying down,
Come quick, quick, that I may lay my head in thy lap.

LADY PERCY

225 Go, ye giddy goose.

The music plays.

HOTSPUR

Now I perceive the Devil understands Welsh,
And 'tis no marvel he is so humorous,
By'r Lady, he is a good musician.

LADY PERCY

Then should you be nothing but musical, for you are alto-
230 gether governed by humours. Lie still, ye thief, and hear the
lady sing in Welsh.

HOTSPUR

I had rather hear Lady, my brach, howl in Irish.

LADY PERCY

Would'st thou have thy head broken?

HOTSPUR

No.

---

219. *book*   agreement.
223. *perfect*   well-skilled. Hotspur may be implying another aspect
of lying down: lovemaking.
227. *humorous*   whimsical.
230. *humours*   emotions (but see II.iv.208, note).
232. *brach*   bitch, presumably of some Irish breed of hunting dog.

LADY PERCY

235   Then be still.

HOTSPUR

Neither!—'tis a woman's fault.

LADY PERCY

Now God help thee!

HOTSPUR [*aside*]

. . . to the Welsh lady's bed.

LADY PERCY

What's that?

HOTSPUR

240   Peace!—she sings.

Here the lady sings a Welsh song.

HOTSPUR

Come, Kate, I'll have your song too.

LADY PERCY

Not mine, in good sooth!

HOTSPUR

Not yours, "in good sooth"! Heart, you swear like a comfit-
maker's wife—"Not you, in good sooth!" and "As true as I
245   live!" and "As God shall mend me!" and "As sure as day!"—
And givest such sarcenet surety for thy oaths,
As if thou never walk'st further than Finsbury.
Swear me, Kate, like a lady as thou art,

---

236. *Neither . . . fault* "I have no more wish to be silent [than to
be hit on the head] because it is effeminate to lack spirit." Some editors
suggest that, for Hotspur, his rejection of both alternatives seems to
show a feminine wilfulness. Again, the passage may contain sexual
overtones.

242. *sooth* truth.

243–4. *comfit-maker* confectioner.

246. *sarcenet* a flimsy silk used for linings in clothes.

247. *Finsbury* Finsbury Fields were a favorite spot for citizens'
recreation, close to London.

A good mouth-filling oath, and leave "in sooth,"
250 And such protest of pepper-gingerbread
To velvet guards, and Sunday citizens.
Come, sing.

LADY PERCY

I will not sing.

HOTSPUR

'Tis the next way to turn tailor, or be redbreast teacher. An the
255 indentures be drawn I'll away within these two hours, and so
come in when ye will.

Exit.

GLENDOWER

Come, come, Lord Mortimer, you are as slow
As hot Lord Percy is on fire to go.
By this our book is drawn; we'll but seal,
And then to horse immediately.

MORTIMER

260   With all my heart.

Exeunt.

[*Scene ii: London, at the King's palace; the day after the robbery at Gadshill.*] *Enter the* KING, PRINCE OF WALES, *and others.*

KING

Lords, give us leave—the Prince of Wales and I
Must have some private conference; but be near at hand,
For we shall presently have need of you.

Exeunt Lords.

---

250. *protest of pepper-gingerbread* swearing of no more substance
than gingerbread.

251. *guards* trimmings (worn on the citizens' wives' finery)—an
example of synechdoche.

254. *'Tis . . . teacher* Hotspur provides her with "reasons" for not
singing. Tailors sang at their work like weavers (II.iv.115–16) but
worked in wretched conditions. Robins needed no teaching. *next*
nearest (hence, quickest).

1. *give us leave* Be so good as to leave us alone.

    I know not whether God will have it so

5   For some displeasing service I have done,

    That in his secret doom out of my blood

    He'll breed revengement and a scourge for me;

    But thou dost in thy passages of life

    Make me believe that thou art only marked

10 For the hot vengeance and the rod of heaven

    To punish my mistreadings. Tell me, else

    Could such inordinate and low desires,

    Such poor, such bare, such lewd, such mean attempts,

    Such barren pleasures, rude society,

15 As thou art matched withal, and grafted to,

    Accompany the greatness of thy blood,

    And hold their level with thy princely heart?

PRINCE

    So please you majesty, I would I could

    Quit all offences with as clear excuse

20 As well as I am doubtless I can purge

    Myself of many I am charged withal;

    Yet such extenuation let me beg

    As, in reproof of many tales devised,

    Which oft the ear of greatness needs must hear

25 By smiling pickthanks, and base newsmongers,

---

   5. *some displeasing service*   In *2HIV*, Henry admits to Hal that he feels guilty about the "indirect crook'd ways I met this crown" (IV.v. 185–6).

   6. *out of my blood*   from my family.

   9–10. *marked . . . heaven*   The lines can mean either that Hal is the only agent assigned as Heaven's scourge for his father's punishment, or, more probably, that Hal himself is made to merit punishment from Heaven only as a means to punish Henry.

   13. *lewd*   low. *attempts*   exploits.

   15. *grafted*   joined, as a cutting is to an alien stem in horticulture.

   19. *Quit*   acquit myself of.

   22–3. *such extenuation . . . devised*   let me receive as much mitigation of guilt from disproving the many invented misdemeanors (as from your pardon for the fewer real offences).

   25. *pickthanks*   flatterers (persons seeking recognition).

I may, for some things true wherein my youth
Hath faulty wandered and irregular,
Find pardon on my true submission.

KING

God pardon thee!—yet let me wonder, Harry,
30 At thy affections, which do hold a wing
Quite from the flight of all thy ancestors.
Thy place in council thou hast rudely lost—
Which by thy younger brother is supplied—
And art almost an alien to the hearts
35 Of all the court and princes of my blood:
The hope and expectation of thy time
Is ruined, and the soul of every man
Prophetically do forethink thy fall.
Had I so lavish of my presence been,
40 So common-hackneyed in the eyes of men,
So stale and cheap to vulgar company,
Opinion, that did help me to the crown,
Had still kept loyal to possession,
And left me in reputeless banishment,
45 A fellow of no mark nor likelihood.
By being seldom seen, I could not stir
But like a comet I was wondered at,
That men would tell their children, "This is he!"
Others would say, "Where? Which is Bolingbroke?"
50 And then I stole all courtesy from heaven,
And dressed myself in such humility

---

28. *submission*   acknowledgment of fault.

30. *affections*   inclinations. *hold a wing*   follow a course.

38. *do*   The verb is plural because of "every man," which implies numbers.

40. *hackneyed*   overused (a "hackney" is a work horse).

42. *Opinion*   public opinion.

43. *possession*   the legal possessor of the crown (i.e., Richard II).

50. *courtesy from heaven*   Kittredge suggests that Henry is thinking of the idea that God treats all men as of equal rank ("God hath no regard of persons," Acts 10:34, Bishops' Bible).

That I did pluck allegiance from men's hearts,
Loud shouts, and salutations from their mouths,
Even in the presence of the crownèd king.
55　Thus did I keep my person fresh and new—
My presence like a robe pontifical,
Ne'er seen but wondered at; and so my state,
Seldom, but sumptuous, showed like a feast,
And won by rareness such solemnity.
60　The skipping king, he ambled up and down,
With shallow jesters, and rash bavin wits,
Soon kindled and soon burnt, carded his state,
Mingled his royalty with cap'ring fools,
Had his great name profanèd with their scorns,
65　And gave his countenance against his name
To laugh at gibing boys, and stand the push
Of every beardless vain comparative—
Grew a companion to the common streets,
Enfeoffed himself to popularity,
70　That, being daily swallowed by men's eyes,
They surfeited with honey, and began to loathe
The taste of sweetness, whereof a little
More than a little is by much too much.

---

56. *pontifical*　papal (one of the Pope's titles is *Pontifex Maximus*, the greatest bridge builder).

57. *state*　pomp, dignity.

58. *Seldom*　used here as an adjective. *feast*　formal celebration of a festival.

59. *won*　wan Qq, an archaic form of the F reading "wonne."

60. *skipping king*　Richard II does not behave as grossly as this in the play *RII*, preceding this one, nor is he so described by Holinshed. *he*　A pronoun was sometimes archaically introduced after a name or noun in Elizabethan English (see p. 168).

61. *bavin*　flashy (a bavin is a fagot of kindling wood).

62. *carded*　In carding, or combing, fine wool was sometimes adulterated with coarser fibre.

65. *against his name*　to the disadvantage of his title as king.

67. *comparative*　maker of satirical comparisons.

69. *Enfeoffed*　a legal term for surrendering possession.

So, when he had occasion to be seen,
75   He was but as the cuckoo is in June—
Heard, not regarded; seen, but with such eyes
As, sick and blunted with community,
Afford no extraordinary gaze
Such as is bent on sun-like majesty
80   When it shines seldom in admiring eyes,
But rather drowsed and hung their eyelids down—
Slept in his face, and rendered such aspect
As cloudy men use to their adversaries—
Being with his presence glutted, gorged, and full.
85   And in that very line, Harry, standest thou,
For thou hast lost thy princely privilege
With vile participation. Not an eye
But is aweary of thy common sight,
Save mine, which hath desired to see thee more,
90   Which now doth that I would not have it do,
Make blind itself with foolish tenderness.

PRINCE

I shall hereafter, my thrice gracious lord,
Be more myself.

KING

For all the world,
As thou art to this hour was Richard then
95   When I from France set foot at Ravenspurgh,
And even as I was then is Percy now.
Now, by my sceptre, and my soul to boot,

---

75. *June*   Though uncommon earlier, by June cuckoos have mi-
grated to England in large numbers.
77. *community*   familiarity.
82. *Slept in*   disregarded (as if asleep).
83. *cloudy*   sullen.
85. *line*   rank, group.
87. *vile participation*   joining low companions.
93. *For all the world*   in the opinion of everyone.
97. *to boot*   as well.

He hath more worthy interest to the state
Than thou the shadow of succession—
100 For, of no right, nor colour like to right,
He doth fill fields with harness in the realm,
Turns head against the lion's armèd jaws,
And, being no more in debt to years than thou,
Leads ancient lords and reverend bishops on
105 To bloody battles, and to bruising arms.
What never-dying honour hath he got
Against renownèd Douglas!—whose high deeds,
Whose hot incursions, and great name in arms,
Holds from all soldiers chief majority
110 And military title capital
Through all the kingdoms that acknowledge Christ.
Thrice hath this Hotspur, Mars in swaddling clothes,
This infant warrior, in his enterprises
Discomfited great Douglas; ta'en him once,
115 Enlargèd him—and made a friend of him
To fill the mouth of deep defiance up,
And shake the peace and safety of our throne.
And what say you to this?—Percy, Northumberland,
The Archbishop's Grace of York, Douglas, Mortimer,

98–9. *more . . . succession*   more claim to participate in government
by his concern for it than you have by trace of legal title.

100. *colour*   pretext.

101. *harness*   armor (here, meaning the soldier who wears it).

102. *Turns head*   directs an army. *lion*   symbolic of kingship.

103. *no more . . . thou*   The historical Hotspur was twenty-three
years older than Hal, and about three years older than Henry IV;
Shakespeare deliberately made him Hal's age instead.

109. *majority*   superiority.

110. *capital*   supreme.

112. *Thrice*   Though an Earl of Douglas was killed in Hotspur's
first encounter, Hotspur himself was captured at the same time and
was later ransomed.

115. *Enlargèd*   freed.

116. *To fill . . . up*   possibly an allusion to the completing of a good
hunting pack by dogs of powerful voice. Theseus, in *MND* (IV.i.

120   Capitulate against us, and are up.
      But wherefore do I tell these news to thee?
      Why, Harry, do I tell thee of my foes,
      Which art my nearest and dearest enemy?
      Thou that art like enough, through vassal fear,
125   Base inclination, and the start of spleen,
      To fight against me under Percy's pay—
      To dog his heels and curtsy at his frowns
      To show how much thou art degenerate.

PRINCE

      Do not think so!—you shall not find it so;
130   And God forgive them that so much have swayed
      Your majesty's good thoughts away from me!
      I will redeem all this on Percy's head,
      And in the closing of some glorious day
      Be bold to tell you that I am your son,
135   When I will wear a garment all of blood,
      And stain my favours in a bloody mask,
      Which, washed away, shall scour my shame with it;
      And that shall be the day, whene'er it lights,
      That this same child of honour and renown,
140   This gallant Hotspur, this all-praisèd knight,
      And your unthought-of Harry chance to meet.
      For every honour sitting on his helm—
      Would they were multitudes, and on my head
      My shames redoubled! For the time will come
145   That I shall make this Northern youth exchange
      His glorious deeds for my indignities.

120–1), claims his hounds are "matched in mouth like bells,/ Each under other."

120. *Capitulate* make an agreement. *up* in revolt.

124. *vassal* servile.

125. *start of spleen* nervous impulse. The spleen was supposed to govern abrupt change of mood; compare V.ii.19, "A hare-brained 'Hotspur,' governed by a spleen."

132. *redeem* expiate and repay. *on* in attacking.

136. *favours* features; but insignia were also called favours.

      Percy is but my factor, good my lord,

      To engross up glorious deeds on my behalf;

      And I will call him to so strict account

150   That he shall render every glory up,

      Yea, even the slightest worship of his time,

      Or I will tear the reckoning from his heart.

      This in the name of God I promise here,

      The which, if He be pleased I shall perform,

155   I do beseech your majesty may salve

      The long-grown wounds of my intemperance;

      If not, the end of life cancels all bonds—

      And I will die a hundred thousand deaths

      Ere break the smallest parcel of this vow.

KING

160   A hundred thousand rebels die in this!

      Thou shalt have charge and sovereign trust herein.

Enter BLUNT.

      How now, good Blunt?—thy looks are full of speed.

BLUNT

      So hath the business that I come to speak of.

      Lord Mortimer of Scotland hath sent word

165   That Douglas and the English rebels met

      The eleventh of this month at Shrewsbury:

---

    147. *factor*   agent.

    148. *engross*   accumulate in bulk.

    150. *render . . . up*   See V.iv.76*ff*.

    151. *worship of his time*   honor won in his lifetime.

    157. *bonds*   bands QqF—an archaic form. It was a proverbial sentiment that "he that dies pays all debts"; see *Temp*, III.ii.140.

    159. *parcel*   part.

    161. *S.D.*   as in F. Qq place it after line 162.

    162. *speed*   urgency.

    164. *Mortimer*   The Scots Earl of March was George Dunbar. Shakespeare mistakenly assumes that his family name would be the same as that of the English Earl of March. Both earls derived their titles from responsibility for frontiers, or "marches."

A mighty and a fearful head they are—
If promises be kept on every hand—
As ever offered foul play in a state.

KING

170 The Earl of Westmoreland set forth today,
With him my son, Lord John of Lancaster—
For this advertisement is five days old.
On Wednesday next, Harry, you shall set forward;
On Thursday we ourselves will march. Our meeting
175 Is Bridgenorth; and, Harry, you shall march
Through Gloucestershire; by which account
Our business valuèd, some twelve days hence
Our general forces at Bridgenorth shall meet.
Our hands are full of business, let's away—
180 Advantage feeds him fat while men delay.

Exeunt.

[*Scene iii: The Boar's Head Tavern, in Eastcheap, later the same day.*] *Enter* FALSTAFF *and* BARDOLPH.

FALSTAFF

Bardolph, am I not fallen away vilely since this last action? Do I not bate? Do I not dwindle? Why, my skin hangs about me like an old lady's loose gown. I am withered like an old applejohn. Well, I'll repent, and that suddenly, while I am in some

---

172. *advertisement* news.
176–7. *by which . . . valuèd* estimating in these terms the time required by our plan.
1. *fallen away vilely* lost weight disgracefully. *last action* the robbery.
2. *bate* abate, grow thin.
3–4. *apple-john* an apple that keeps well, though the skin shrivels. *OED* says the name comes from the fact that such apples ripen long after the picking date—some even about St. John's Day (June 24) of the next year, just before the new crop (see "Old Apples," *The Times*, London, May 13, 1964). *suddenly* immediately.

5　　liking; I shall be out of heart shortly, and then I shall have no
　　strength to repent. And I have not forgotten what the inside
　　of a church is made of, I am a peppercorn, a brewer's horse!
　　The inside of a church!—company, villainous company hath
　　been the spoil of me!

BARDOLPH

10　Sir John, you are so fretful you cannot live long.

FALSTAFF

Why, there is it!—come, sing me a bawdy song, make me
merry. I was as virtuously given as a gentleman need to be,
virtuous enough: swore little; diced not above seven times—
a week; went to a bawdy house not above once in a quarter—
15　of an hour; paid money that I borrowed—three or four times;
lived well, and in good compass; and now I live out of all
order, out of all compass.

BARDOLPH

Why, you are so fat, Sir John, that you must needs be out of
all compass, out of all reasonable compass, Sir John.

FALSTAFF

20　Do thou amend thy face, and I'll amend my life; thou art our
admiral, thou bearest the lantern in the poop—but 'tis in the

---

　　5. *liking*　inclination, also perhaps "in good shape" (R. Cotgrave's
Dictionary, 1611: "somewhat fat, in pretty good liking"). *out of heart*
depressed.

　　7. *peppercorn*　the dry shriveled berry from which pepper is made.
brewer's horse　compare Dekker's *If this be not a Good Play*, III.i.
10–11 (Bowers, III,162): "as noblemen use their great horses, when
they are past service: sell 'em to brewers and make 'em dray-horses."
See also II.iv.167, note.

　　12. *given*　inclined.

　　14. *quarter*　The business year in England, as in the United States,
is broken into four quarters.

　　16. *in good compass*　within the circumference, or limits of decorum.

　　21. *admiral . . . poop*　The admiral's flagship led a fleet at night by
means of a lantern set on its high stern (hence the pun, in the next
line, on the nautical sense of *nose*: a ship's stem).

nose of thee: thou art the Knight of the Burning Lamp.

BARDOLPH

Why, Sir John, my face does you no harm.

FALSTAFF

No, I'll be sworn, I make as good use of it as many a man doth
25   of a death's-head, or a *memento mori*. I never see thy face, but
I think upon hell fire, and Dives that lived in purple—for there
he is in his robes, burning, burning. If thou wert any way
given to virtue, I would swear by thy face: my oath should be
"By this fire, that's God's angel!" But thou art altogether given
30   over, and wert indeed, but for the light in thy face, the son of
utter darkness. When thou ran'st up Gad's Hill in the night to
catch my horse, if I did not think thou hadst been an *ignis
fatuus*, or a ball of wildfire, there's no purchase in money. O
thou art a perpetual triumph, an everlasting bonfire-light!
35   Thou hast saved me a thousand marks in links and torches,
walking with thee in the night betwixt tavern and tavern; but
the sack that thou hast drunk me would have bought me lights
as good cheap at the dearest chandler's in Europe. I have main-

---

22. *Knight . . . Lamp*   a parody of knights' titles in romances, the
names being taken from the heraldic devices on their shields.

25. *death's head*   The use of a skull motif as a pious reminder of
human mortality (*memento mori*) was common on ornaments.

26. *Dives*   the rich man doomed to suffer in hell after a happy life,
while Lazarus the beggar went to heaven (Luke 14:19–31).

29. *By . . . angel*   Compare Psalm 104:4 (Bishops' Bible): "Who
maketh his angels spirits; his ministers a flaming fire." The same oath
appears in an old play, *Misogonus* (1570).

29–30. *given over*   given up as irredeemably wicked.

32–3. *ignis fatuus*   the spontaneous combustion of marsh gases,
also called "will o' the wisp." *ball of wildfire*   a form of lightning—
also applied to a burning bundle of explosives. Perhaps suggested by
"wildfire" as another name for erysipelas (a skin disease producing
red discoloration).

34. *triumph*   festival or parade (with torches or fireworks).

35. *marks*   A mark was worth two-thirds of a pound. *links*   a
torch made of tow and pitch.

38. *as good cheap*   with no more expense.

40 tained that salamander of yours with fire any time this two and
    thirty years, God reward me for it!

BARDOLPH

'Sblood, I would my face were in your belly!

FALSTAFF

God-a-mercy! so should I be sure to be heartburnt.

Enter Hostess

How now, Dame Partlet the hen? Have you inquired yet who
picked my pocket?

HOSTESS

45 Why, Sir John, what do think, Sir John—do you think I keep
    thieves in my house? I have searched, I have inquired, so has
    my husband, man by man, boy by boy, servant by servant—
    the tithe of a hair was never lost in my house before.

FALSTAFF

Ye lie, hostess—Bardolph was shaved, and lost many a hair,
50 and I'll be sworn my pocket was picked; go to, you are a
    woman, go.

HOSTESS

Who, I? No!—I defy thee; God's light, I was never called so
in my own house before.

FALSTAFF

Go to, I know you well enough.

---

39. *salamander*   A lizard supposed to be able to live in fire because
of its cold blood, according to the classical zoologist Pliny (*Natural
History*, X.lxxxvi).

41. *in your belly*   that is, not on your tongue (compare "eat one's
words").

42. *God-a-mercy*   God have mercy.

43. *Dame Partlet the hen*   The hen Pertelote appears in *The Nun's
Priest's Tale* of Chaucer. Mistress Quickly's bustling, flustered manner
presumably suggests Pertelote's domination of her Chanticleer.

48. *tithe*   tenth part. QqF have "tight"—perhaps derived from a
mispelling, such as "tihte" (unless it is a Quicklyism).

52. *God's light*   daylight: a common oath.

HOSTESS

55   No, Sir John; you do not know me, Sir John—I know you, Sir
John: you owe me money, Sir John, and now you pick a quarrel
to beguile me of it. I bought you a dozen of shirts to your back.

FALSTAFF

Dowlas, filthy dowlas. I have given them away to bakers'
wives; they have made bolters of them.

HOSTESS

60   Now, as I am a true woman—holland of eight shillings an ell!
You owe money here besides, Sir John, for your diet, and by-
drinkings, and money lent you, four and twenty pound.

FALSTAFF

He had his part of it, let him pay.

HOSTESS

He?—alas, he is poor, he hath nothing.

FALSTAFF

65   How? Poor!—look upon his face. What call you rich? Let them
coin his nose, let them coin his cheeks—I'll not pay a denier.
What, will you make a younker of me? Shall I not take mine
ease in mine inn but I shall have my pocket picked? I have lost
a seal-ring of my grandfather's worth forty mark.

HOSTESS

70   O Jesu, I have heard the prince tell him, I know not how oft,
that that ring was copper.

FALSTAFF

How?—the prince is a Jack, a sneak-up. 'Sblood, and he were
here I would cudgel him like a dog if he would say so.

---

58. *Dowlas*   coarse linen named for Daoulas, near Brest in Brittany.
59. *bolters*   cloths for sifting flour.
60. *holland*   linen with a fine finish, first made in the Netherlands.
ell   forty-five inches.
61–2. *by-drinkings*   drinks between meals.
66. *denier*   a French copper coin of small value.
67. *younker*   young greenhorn, or victim.
72. *Jack*   rascal. *sneak-up*   sly rogue.

Enter the PRINCE *marching,* [*with* PETO;] *and* FALSTAFF
meets him, playing upon his truncheon like a fife.

FALSTAFF

How now, lad? Is the wind in that door, i'faith—must we all
75   march?

BARDOLPH

Yea, two and two, Newgate fashion.

HOSTESS

My lord, I pray you hear me.

PRINCE

What say'st thou, Mistress Quickly? How doth thy husband?
I love him well, he is an honest man.

HOSTESS

80   Good my lord, hear me!

FALSTAFF

Prithee let her alone, and list to me.

PRINCE

What say'st thou, Jack?

FALSTAFF

The other night I fell asleep here, behind the arras, and had my
pocket picked—this house is turned bawdy-house, they pick
85   pockets.

PRINCE

What didst thou lose, Jack?

FALSTAFF

Wilt thou believe me, Hal, three or four bonds of forty pound
apiece, and a seal-ring of my grandfather's.

PRINCE

A trifle, some eightpenny matter.

---

74. *Is . . . door*   Is that the way the wind is blowing?
76. *Newgate fashion*   linked together in pairs like prisoners going
to and from Newgate jail.

HOSTESS

90 So I told him, my lord, and I said I heard your grace say so;
    and, my lord, he speaks most vilely of you, like a foul-mouthed
    man as he is, and said he would cudgel you.

PRINCE

What?—he did not?

HOSTESS

There's neither faith, truth, nor womanhood in me else.

FALSTAFF

95 There's no more faith in thee than in a stewed prune, nor no
    more truth in thee than in a drawn fox, and for womanhood—
    Maid Marion may be the deputy's wife of the ward to thee. Go,
    you thing, go!

HOSTESS

Say, what thing? What thing?

FALSTAFF

100 What thing?—why a thing to thank God on.

HOSTESS

I am no thing to thank God on, I would thou shouldst know it!
I am an honest man's wife, and setting thy knighthood aside,
thou art a knave to call me so.

FALSTAFF

Setting thy womanhood aside, thou art a beast to say other-
105 wise.

---

95. *stewed prune* a symbol for a bawd, as prunes were often displayed in brothels (compare Dekker, *2 Honest Whore*, IV.iii.36;
Bowers, II,197: "two dishes of stewed prunes, a bawd and a pander").
    96. *drawn* from cover, and forced to rely on guile to escape
hunters.
    97. *Maid Marion* an indecorous female role in the May Day Mor-
ris dances, often played by a man. *deputy* an official of some dignity
in local administration. *to* compared to.
    100. *on* for. Falstaff's phrase only appears to be insulting; Mis-
tress Quickly actually slanders herself by reversing it, as Falstaff
points out.

HOSTESS

Say, what beast, thou knave, thou?

FALSTAFF

What beast?—why, an otter.

PRINCE

An otter, Sir John! Why an otter?

FALSTAFF

Why?—she's neither fish nor flesh, a man knows not where
110 to have her.

HOSTESS

Thou art an unjust man in saying so; thou or any man knows
where to have me, thou knave, thou!

PRINCE

Thou say'st true, hostess, and he slanders thee most grossly.

HOSTESS

So doth he you, my lord, and said this other day you ought
115 him a thousand pound.

PRINCE

Sirrah, do I owe you a thousand pound?

FALSTAFF

A thousand pound, Hal?—a million! Thy love is worth a million; thou owest me thy love.

HOSTESS

Nay, my lord, he called you Jack, and said he would cudgel
120 you.

FALSTAFF

Did I, Bardolph?

---

107. *otter*   Compare Shirley, *The Grateful Servant*, II.i: "otters, appear flesh, but really are fish."

109–10. *where . . . her*   how to deal with her; but the phrase vul-
garly carried the meaning of having intercourse, so the Hostess in
reply inadvertently slanders herself.

114. *ought*   owed (an archaism).

BARDOLPH

Indeed, Sir John, you said so.

FALSTAFF

Yea, if he said my ring was copper.

PRINCE

I say 'tis copper; darest thou be as good as thy word now?

FALSTAFF

125 Why, Hal, thou knowest as thou art but a man I dare, but as
thou art prince, I fear thee as I fear the roaring of the lion's
whelp.

PRINCE

And why not as the lion?

FALSTAFF

The king himself is to be feared as the lion—dost thou think
130 I'll fear thee as I fear thy father? Nay, and I do, I pray God
my girdle break.

PRINCE

O, if it should, how would thy guts fall about thy knees! But
sirrah, there's no room for faith, truth, nor honesty in this
bosom of thine. It is all filled up with guts and midriff. Charge
135 an honest woman with picking thy pocket! Why, thou whoreson, impudent, embossed rascal, if there were anything in thy
pocket but tavern reckonings, memorandums of bawdy houses,
and one poor pennyworth of sugar-candy to make thee longwinded, if thy pocket were enriched with any other injuries

---

131. *girdle* Belts were often symbols of honor (compare "a belted
earl"). Falstaff's invocation was therefore conventional.

136. *embossed* bloated; but in venery it also meant "foaming at
the mouth" (*The Noble Art of Venery*, 1570), and *rascal* was also a
technical term for a deer of poor quality, so a pun may be intended.

138–9. *sugar . . . longwinded* a contemporary medical theory, perhaps related to the energizing properties of sugar.

139. *injuries* sources of distress (by their disappearance), but perhaps with an offensive bearing on the things themselves, as the end of
the sentence implies.

140 but these, I am a villain—and yet you will stand to it, you will
not pocket up wrong. Art thou not ashamed?

FALSTAFF

Dost thou hear, Hal? Thou knowest in the state of innocency
Adam fell, and what should poor Jack Falstaff do in the days
of villainy? Thou seest I have more flesh than another man,
145 and therefore more frailty. You confess then, you picked my
pocket?

PRINCE

It appears so by the story.

FALSTAFF

Hostess, I forgive thee—go make ready breakfast, love thy
husband, look to thy servants, cherish thy guests; thou shalt
150 find me tractable to any honest reason—thou seest I am pacified still; nay, prithee be gone. (*Exit* Hostess.) Now, Hal, to the
news at court: for the robbery, lad, how is that answered?

PRINCE

O, my sweet beef, I must still be good angel to thee—the
money is paid back again.

FALSTAFF

155 O, I do not like that paying back, 'tis a double labour.

PRINCE

I am good friends with my father and may do anything.

FALSTAFF

Rob me the exchequer the first thing thou dost, and do it with
unwashed hands too.

BARDOLPH

Do, my lord.

144–5. *flesh . . . frailty* Compare Matthew 26:41: "The flesh is
weak"; colloquially, this was often modified to the alliterative "flesh
is frail," as in Peele's *Edward I*, scene vii.
150–51. *am pacified still* can always be pacified.
153. *beef* ox.
157–8. *with . . . hands* at once (without concern for decorum).

PRINCE

160　I have procured thee, Jack, a charge of foot.

FALSTAFF

I would it had been of horse. Where shall I find one that can
steal well? O for a fine thief of the age of two and twenty or
thereabouts—I am heinously unprovided. Well, God be
thanked for these rebels, they offend none but the virtuous; I
165　laud them, I praise them.

PRINCE

Bardolph!

BARDOLPH

My lord?

PRINCE

Go bear this letter to Lord John of Lancaster—
To my brother John; this to my Lord of Westmoreland.

[*Exit* BARDOLPH.]

170　Go, Peto, to horse, to horse—for thou and I
Have thirty miles to ride yet ere dinner-time.

[*Exit* PETO.]

Jack, meet me tomorrow in the Temple Hall
At two o'clock in the afternoon;
There shalt thou know thy charge, and there receive
175　Money and order for their furniture.
The land is burning; Percy stands on high;
And either we or they must lower lie.

[*Exit.*]

FALSTAFF

Rare words! Brave world! Hostess, my breakfast, come!
Oh, I could wish this tavern were my drum.

[*Exit.*]

---

160. *charge of foot*　an infantry command.
163. *unprovided*　without equipment for soldiering.
172. *Temple Hall*　one of the lawyers' Inns of Court, in London.
175. *furniture*　equipment.
179. *drum*　Drums rallied troops to battle. *NCS* suggests a pun on
"tavern" (Lat. *taberna*) and "tabor" or "tabern" (a nonmilitary drum).

[*Act IV, scene i: Some time later, at the rebel camp near Shrewsbury. Enter* HOTSPUR, WORCESTER, *and* DOUGLAS.]

HOTSPUR

Well said, my noble Scot! If speaking truth
In this fine age were not thought flattery,
Such attribution should the Douglas have
As not a soldier of this season's stamp
5 Should go so general current through the world.
By God, I cannot flatter, I do defy
The tongues of soothers—but a braver place
In my heart's love hath no man than yourself;
Nay, task me to my word, approve me, lord.

DOUGLAS

10 Thou art the King of Honour.
No man so potent breathes upon the ground
But I will beard him.

HOTSPUR

Do so, and 'tis well—

Enter one with letters.

What letters hast thou there?—I can but thank you.

MESSENGER

These letters come from your father.

HOTSPUR

15 Letters from him!—why comes he not himself?

---

3. *attribution*   ascription of (good) qualities.
4–5. *stamp . . . current*   The images are derived from coin minting.
6. *defy*   repudiate.
7. *soothers*   flatterers. *braver*   more honorable.
9. *task . . . approve me*   put my words to proof by some task.
12. *beard*   meet face to face (in fight, or defiance).
13. The first part of the line is to the messenger, the second to Douglas. Qq put S.D. after Douglas' speech.

MESSENGER

He cannot come, my lord; he is grievous sick.

HOTSPUR

'Zounds, how has he the leisure to be sick
In such a justling time? Who leads his power?
Under whose government come they along?

MESSENGER

20   His letters bear his mind, not I, my lord.

WORCESTER

I prithee tell me, doth he keep his bed?

MESSENGER

He did, my lord, four days ere I set forth,
And at the time of my departure thence
He was much feared by his physicians.

WORCESTER

25   I would the state of time had first been whole
Ere he by sickness had been visited.
His health was never better worth than now.

HOTSPUR

Sick now!—droop now!—this sickness doth infect
The very life-blood of our enterprise;
30   'Tis catching hither even to our camp.
He writes me here that inward sickness . . .
And that his friends by deputation could not

---

18. *justling*   busily active.

20. Q1 reads "His letters beares his mind, not I my mind." Q7 reads
"bear." Qq3–5,F have "I his mind." Capell's edn. plausibly suggests
that the problem began with a compositor's mistake—he repeated the
earlier "mind," when his copy actually read "I, my lord"—and the
later editions then "corrected" this by changing the pronoun.

24. *feared*   feared for.

25. *whole*   healthy (i.e., without the disease of war).

31. *sickness* . . .   Presumably, Hotspur breaks off to give the more
serious information that follows.

32. *deputation*   deputies.

So soon be drawn, nor did he think it meet
To lay so dangerous and dear a trust
35   On any soul removed, but on his own.
Yet doth he give us bold advertisement,
That with our small conjunction we should on,
To see how fortune is disposed to us;
For, as he writes, there is no quailing now,
40   Because the king is certainly possessed
Of all our purposes. What say you to it?

WORCESTER

Your father's sickness is a maim to us.

HOTSPUR

A perilous gash, a very limb lopped off—
And yet, in faith, it is not! His present want
45   Seems more than we shall find it. Were it good
To set the exact wealth of all our states
All at one cast?—to set so rich a main
On the nice hazard of one doubtful hour?
It were not good, for therein should we read
50   The very bottom and the soul of hope,
The very list, the very utmost bound
Of all our fortunes.

DOUGLAS

Faith, and so we should—

---

33. *drawn*   drawn together.
35. *any . . . removed*   any outsider.
36. *advertisement*   advice.
37. *conjunction*   united force.
40. *possessed*   informed.
44. *His . . . want*   the lack of him now.
46–8. *set . . . cast . . . main . . . hazard*   gambling terms—a main was a stake, but could mean "army."
50. *soul*   ultimate nature (also perhaps a pun on "sole").
51. *list*   schedule; or boundary (literally, the edge of a piece of cloth).
53. *reversiòn*   (four syllables) future inheritance.

Where now remains a sweet reversiòn.
We may boldly spend, upon the hope
55 Of what is to come in . . .
A comfort of retirement lives in this.

HOTSPUR

A rendezvous, a home to fly unto
If that the Devil and Mischance look big
Upon the maidenhead of our affairs.

WORCESTER

60 But yet I would your father had been here:
The quality and hair of our attempt
Brooks no division—it will be thought
By some that know not why he is away
That wisdom, loyalty, and mere dislike
65 Of our proceedings kept the earl from hence;
And think how such an apprehension
May turn the tide of fearful faction,
And breed a kind of question in our cause;
For well you know we of the off'ring side
70 Must keep aloof from strict arbitrement,
And stop all sight-holes, every loop from whence
The eye of Reason may pry in upon us—
This absence of your father's draws a curtain

54–5. as F; one line in Qq. The short line suggests a doubtful pause.
56. *retirement* a place to retire to.
58. *big* threateningly.
59. *maidenhead* immature condition.
61. *hair* complexion, nature.
62. *Brooks* tolerates.
64. *mere* pure.
66. *apprehension* Originally, this meant simply "idea."
67. *fearful* timorous.
69. *off'ring* challenging, taking the offensive.
70. *strict arbitrement* precise evaluation.
71. *loop* loop-hole.

That shows the ignorant a kind of fear
Before not dreamt of.

HOTSPUR

75   You strain too far.
I rather of his absence make this use:
It lends a lustre and more great opinion,
A larger dare to our great enterprise
Than if the earl were here; for men must think
80   If we without his help can make a head
To push against a kingdom, with his help
We shall o'erturn it topsy-turvy down.
Yet all goes well, yet all our joints are whole.

DOUGLAS

85   As heart can think! There is not such a word
Spoke in Scotland as this term of "fear."

Enter SIR RICHARD VERNON.

HOTSPUR

My cousin Vernon!—welcome, by my soul!

VERNON

Pray God my news be worth a welcome, lord—
The Earl of Westmoreland, seven thousand strong,
Is marching hitherwards, with him Prince John.

HOTSPUR

No harm!—what more!

VERNON

90   And further, I have learned
The king himself in person is set forth,
Or hitherwards intended speedily,
With strong and mighty preparation.

---

75. *strain*   exaggerate.
77. *opinion*   reputation.
80. *make a head*   raise an army.

HOTSPUR

He shall be welcome too! Where is his son?—
95　The nimble-footed madcap Prince of Wales,
　　And his comrades that daffed the world aside
　　And bid it pass.

VERNON

　　　　　　　　All furnished, all in arms,
　　All plumed, like estridges that with the wind
　　Bated; like eagles having lately bathed;
100　Glittering in golden coats like images;
　　As full of spirit as the month of May,
　　And gorgeous as the sun at Midsummer;
　　Wanton as youthful goats, wild as young bulls.
　　I saw young Harry with his beaver on,
105　His cushes on his thighs, gallantly armed,
　　Rise from the ground like feathered Mercury,
　　And vaulted with such ease into his seat
　　As if an angel dropped down from the clouds

---

96. *daffed* threw (variant of *doff*).

97. *pass* go its own way; a reveler's exclamation (compare N.
Udall, *Ralph Roister Doister*, III.iii.42: "Be of good cheer, man, and let
the world pass!").

98–9. *estridges . . . bated* The imagery of the whole speech derives
from Nashe's *Unfortunate Traveller* (McKerrow, II, 272), which clarifies the meaning as follows: the (ostrich) plumes on the knights' hel-
mets flutter like ostrich wings beating the air ("bated," a falconry term,
comes from the French *battre*, to beat) when the birds are excited, but
not flying. The passage is much discussed editorially—Rowe (unnec-
essarily) emended it to "wing the wind,/ Bated" and this is accepted
by *NCS*. Less plausibly, Douce argues that *estridge* is used in its possible sense of "goshawk"; but the crest of the Prince of Wales is
formed of ostrich plumes. Another source for some details is Spenser's
Faerie Queene, I.xi.34.

100. *images* religious statues, which often bear elaborate robes.

103. *wanton* sportive.

104. *beaver* helmet.

105. *cushes* cuisses, thigh armor; their weight emphasizes Hal's
agility in mounting his horse.

To turn and wind a fiery Pegasus,
110   And witch the world with noble horsemanship.

HOTSPUR

No more, no more!—worse than the sun in March,
This praise doth nourish agues. Let them come!
They come like sacrifices in their trim,
And to the fire-eyed maid of smoky war
115   All hot and bleeding will we offer them;
The mailèd Mars shall on his altars sit
Up to the ears in blood. I am on fire
To hear this rich reprisal is so nigh
And yet not ours—come, let me taste my horse,
120   Who is to bear me like a thunderbolt
Against the bosom of the Prince of Wales.
Harry to Harry shall, hot horse to horse,
Meet and ne'er part till one drop down a corse.
O that Glendower were come!

VERNON

There is more news:
125   I learned in Worcester as I rode along
He cannot draw his power this fourteen days.

DOUGLAS

That's the worst tidings that I hear of yet.

---

109. *wind . . . Pegasus*   maneuver a horse as lively as the mythical
flying horse Pegasus.

110. *witch*   bewitch (see p. 169).

112. *agues*   Fevers were supposed to be encouraged by the mists
raised by the sun, especially in the spring (compare *Lear*, II.iv.164*ff.*).

113. *trim*   Animals prepared for sacrifice were garlanded with
flowers, etc.

114. *fire-eyed maid*   Bellona was the goddess of war.

118. *reprisal*   prize.

119. *taste*   test (from the French *tâter*, to try).

123. *corse*   a common spelling of "corpse."

126. *cannot*   Q5,F. Q1–4 (and uncorrected copies of Q5) read *can*.
draw   muster. Shakespeare follows Daniel here, not Holinshed, who
says the Welsh were present.

127. *yet*   Q5,F. Q1–4, Q5 (uncorrected) read *it*.

WORCESTER

Ay, by my faith, that bears a frosty sound.

HOTSPUR

What may the king's whole battle reach unto?

VERNON

To thirty thousand.

HOTSPUR

130　　　　　　　　　　Forty let it be!
My father and Glendower being both away,
The powers of us may serve so great a day.
Come let us take a muster speedily,
Doomsday is near—die all, die merrily!

DOUGLAS

135　Talk not of dying—I am out of fear
Of death or death's hand for this one half year.

　　　　　　　　　　　　　　　　　　Exeunt.

[*Scene ii: About the same time, on a road near Coventry.*]
Enter FALSTAFF, BARDOLPH.

FALSTAFF

Bardolph, get thee before to Coventry, fill me a bottle of sack;
our soldiers shall march through: we'll to Sutton Co'fil' tonight.

BARDOLPH

Will you give me money, captain?

FALSTAFF

Lay out, lay out.

---

129. *battle*　army.
134. *merrily*　Q2–5,F. Q1 reads *merely*.
2. *Sutton Co'fil'*　Qq: "Sutton Cophill"; Sutton Coldfield is in
Warwickshire near Coventry.
4. *Lay out*　Pay it yourself.

BARDOLPH

5   This bottle makes an angel.

FALSTAFF

And if it do, take it for thy labour—and if it make twenty, take them all; I'll answer the coinage. Bid my lieutenant Peto meet me at town's end.

BARDOLPH

I will, captain. Farewell.   *Exit.*

FALSTAFF

10 If I be not ashamed of my soldiers, I am a soused gurnet—I have misused the king's press damnably. I have got, in exchange of a hundred and fifty soldiers, three hundred and odd pounds. I press me none but good householders, yeomen's sons, inquire me out contracted bachelors, such as had been

15 asked twice on the banns: such a commodity of warm slaves as had as lief hear the Devil as a drum, such as fear the report of a caliver worse than a struck fowl or a hurt wild duck. I pressed me none but such toasts-and-butter, with hearts in their bellies no bigger than pins' heads—and they have bought out their

20 services; and now my whole charge consists of ancients, cor-

---

5. *makes an angel*   increases the money you owe me to the value of one angel-noble (a gold coin stamped with the figure of the Archangel Michael, and worth a third of a pound, or more).

7. *answer the coinage*   accept the responsibility (with an allusion to counterfeiting).

10. *soused gurnet*   a pickled small fish, eaten as a delicacy, like anchovies.

11. *misused . . . press*   abused the right of the king to conscript soldiers.

14. *contracted*   engaged to be married (the marriage takes place after inquiries for any impediments have been made in church on three Sundays—the asking of the banns).

15. *commodity*   batch.   *warm slaves*   comfortably situated cowards.

17. *caliver*   musket.

18. *toasts-and-butter*   delicate eaters.

19–20. *bought . . . services*   paid money to be replaced.

20. *ancients*   ensigns (originally, standard bearers).

porals, lieutenants, gentlemen of companies—slaves as ragged
as Lazarus in the painted cloth where the glutton's dogs licked
his sores, and such as indeed were never soldiers but discarded
unjust servingmen, younger sons to younger brothers, revolted
25 tapsters, and ostlers trade-fallen—the cankers of a calm world
and a long peace, ten times more dishonorable ragged than an
old fazed ancient; and such have I to fill up the rooms of them
as have bought out their services, that you would think that I
had a hundred and fifty tattered prodigals lately come from
30 swine-keeping, from eating draff and husks. A mad fellow met
me on the way, and told me I had unloaded all the gibbets and
pressed the dead bodies. No eye hath seen such scarecrows. I'll
not march through Coventry with them, that's flat; nay, and
the villains march wide betwixt the legs as if they had gyves
35 on, for indeed I had the most of them out of prison—there's
not a shirt and a half in all my company, and the half shirt is
two napkins tacked together and thrown over the shoulders

---

21. *gentlemen of companies*   These ranked above private soldiers
of the conscript kind; like the other officers mentioned, they were vol-
unteers. All of Falstaff's company are the poorest outcasts, but are
enrolled in the higher ranks; Falstaff steals their extra pay, according
to *NCS*.

22. *painted cloth*   a cheap substitute for tapestry wall hangings;
Falstaff alludes to the same biblical scene at III.iii.27.

24. *revolted*   runaway (compare II.iv.40ff.).

25. *trade-fallen*   unemployed. *cankers*   parasites; fostered by political inactivity according to Elizabethan sociology: compare Bacon's
essay *Of the True Greatness of Kingdoms*, "No body can be healthful
without exercise, neither natural body nor politic."

26. *dishonorable*   used adverbially.

27. *fazed ancient*   unraveled flag—whose rags are honorable, in
contrast to those of Falstaff's men. F reads "old fac'd ancient" (see
note, line 22), which is often followed.

29–30. *prodigals . . . husks*   another typically Falstaffian biblical allusion, to the parable of the prodigal son (Luke 15); *husks* is taken
from the Geneva translation; *draff* is pig-swill.

34. *gyves*   fetters.

35. *out of prison*   NCS notes that prisoners were enlisted in 1596
for the Cadiz expedition.

like a herald's coat without sleeves; and the shirt, to say the
truth, stolen from my host at St. Albans, or the red-nose inn-
40   keeper at Daventry. But that's all one—they'll find linen
enough on every hedge.

Enter the PRINCE [*and the*] LORD OF WESTMORELAND

PRINCE

How now, blown Jack? How now quilt?

FALSTAFF

What, Hal! How now, mad wag? What a devil dost thou in
Warwickshire? My good Lord Westmoreland, I cry you mercy
45   —I thought your honour had already been at Shrewsbury.

WESTMORELAND

Faith, Sir John, 'tis more than time that I were there, and you
too, but my powers are there already. The king, I can tell you,
looks for us all—we must away all night.

FALSTAFF

Tut, never fear me; I am as vigilant as a cat to steal cream.

PRINCE

50   I think, to steal cream indeed, for thy theft hath already made
thee butter. But tell me, Jack, whose fellows are these that
come after?

FALSTAFF

Mine, Hal, mine.

PRINCE

I did never see such pitiful rascals.

---

40. *that's all one*   that makes no difference.
41. *on every hedge*   where linen was spread to dry or bleach in the
sun.
42. *blown . . . quilt*   "blown" is a quibble—"puffed up," and
"breathless." A "jack" was also a soldier's padded tunic, hence "quilt."
43. *mad wag*   wild wit.
44. *cry you mercy*   beg your pardon (for not seeing you).
49. *fear me*   fear for my performance.

FALSTAFF

55 Tut, tut, good enough to toss, food for powder, food for powder—they'll fill a pit as well as better; tush man, mortal men,
mortal men.

WESTMORELAND

Ay, but Sir John, methinks they are exceeding poor and bare—
too beggarly.

FALSTAFF

60 Faith, for their poverty, I know not where they had that; and
for their bareness, I am sure they never learned that of me.

PRINCE

No, I'll be sworn, unless thou call three fingers in the ribs bare.
But sirrah, make haste—Percy is already in the field.

Exit.

FALSTAFF

What, is the king encamped?

WESTMORELAND

65 He is, Sir John. I fear we shall stay too long.

FALSTAFF [*aside*]

Well, to the latter end of a fray and the beginning of a feast,
fits a dull fighter and a keen guest.

Exeunt.

[*Scene iii: The rebel camp near Shrewsbury.*] *Enter* HOTSPUR,
WORCESTER, DOUGLAS, VERNON.

HOTSPUR

We'll fight with him tonight.

WORCESTER

It may not be.

---

55. *toss* with pikes.
62. *fingers* A finger equals three-fourths of an inch.
66–7. *to . . . guest* a common proverb.

DOUGLAS

You give him then advantage.

VERNON

                                        Not a whit.

HOTSPUR

Why say you so?—looks he not for supply?

VERNON

So do we.

HOTSPUR

                    His is certain, ours is doubtful.

WORCESTER

5   Good cousin, be advised; stir not tonight.

VERNON

Do not, my lord.

DOUGLAS

                              You do not counsel well;
You speak it out of fear, and cold heart.

VERNON

Do me no slander, Douglas. By my life—
And I dare well maintain it with my life—
10   If well-respected honour bid me on,
I hold as little counsel with weak fear
As you, my lord, or any Scot that this day lives;
Let it be seen tomorrow in the battle
Which of us fears.

DOUGLAS

                              Yea, or tonight.

VERNON

                                        Content.

---

3. *supply*   reinforcements.

10. *well-respected*   approved by experienced authorities. *bid me on*   call upon me to go on.

HOTSPUR

15   Tonight, say I.

VERNON

Come, come, it may not be. I wonder much,
Being men of such great leading as you are,
That you forsee not what impediments
Drag back our expedition: certain horse
20   Of my cousin Vernon's are not yet come up;
Your uncle Worcester's horse came but today,
And now their pride and mettle is asleep,
Their courage with hard labour tame and dull,
That not a horse is half the half of himself.

HOTSPUR

25   So are the horses of the enemy
In general journey-bated and brought low—
The better part of ours are full of rest.

WORCESTER

The number of the king exceedeth ours.
For God's sake, cousin, stay till all come in.

                              The trumpet sounds a parley.

Enter SIR WALTER BLUNT.

BLUNT

30   I come with gracious offers from the king,
If you vouchsafe me hearing and respect.

---

17. *such great leading*   such skill in leadership.

19. *Drag . . . expedition*   restrain our haste. *horse*   cavalry.

21. *horse*   Q5,F. Q1–4 read *horses.* The plural breaks the meter.

24. Most editors find this line reads falsely. Pope's edn. drops *the*; Steevens' drops *of.*

26. *journey-bated*   fatigued (abated) by travel.

28. *ours*   Q6,F. Q1–4 read *our*—a possible archaism, according to *OED.*

29. S.D.   Shakespeare replaces Holinshed's anonymous clerical ambassadors with Blunt.

HOTSPUR

Welcome, Sir Walter Blunt; and would to God
You were of our determination!
Some of us love you well, and even those some
35   Envy your great deservings and good name,
Because you are not of our quality,
But stand against us like an enemy.

BLUNT

And God defend but still I should stand so,
So long as out of limit and true rule
40   You stand against anointed majesty.
But to my charge. The king hath sent to know
The nature of your griefs, and whereupon
You conjure from the breast of civil Peace
Such bold hostility, teaching his duteous land
45   Audacious cruelty. If that the king
Have any way your good deserts forgot,
Which he confesseth to be manifold,
He bids you name your griefs; and with all speed
You shall have your desires with interest
50   And pardon absolute for yourself, and these
Herein misled by your suggestion.

HOTSPUR

The king is kind, and well we know the king
Knows at what time to promise, when to pay:
My father, and my uncle, and myself

---

33. *determination*   point of view.
35. *Envy*   grudge.
36. *quality*   party (often used in a professional sense: the outlaws in *2Gent.* try to win Valentine for their gang as "a man of such perfection/ As we do in our quality much want." IV.i.57–8).
38. *defend*   forbid (compare French *défendre*).
39. *limit*   bounds of propriety.
41. *charge*   the duty with which I am charged.
51. *suggestion*   used with a sinister sense (compare *Lear*, II.i.73: "suggestion, plot, and damned practice").

55   Did give him that same royalty he wears,
      And when he was not six and twenty strong,
      Sick in the world's regard, wretched and low,
      A poor unminded outlaw sneaking home,
      My father gave him welcome to the shore;
60   And when he heard him swear and vow to God
      He came but to be Duke of Lancaster—
      To sue his livery, and beg his peace
      With tears of innocency and terms of zeal—
      My father, in kind heart and pity moved,
65   Swore him assistance, and performed it too.
      Now when the lords and barons of the realm
      Perceived Northumberland did lean to him,
      The more and less came in with cap and knee,
      Met him in boroughs, cities, villages,
70   Attended him on bridges, stood in lanes,
      Laid gifts before him, proffered him their oaths,
      Gave him their heirs as pages, followed him
      Even at the heels in golden multitudes.
      He presently, as greatness knows itself,
75   Steps me a little higher than his vow
      Made to my father while his blood was poor
      Upon the naked shore at Ravenspurgh—
      And now, forsooth, takes on him to reform

---

62. *livery*   the legal delivery of lands (due him as heir of John of Gaunt, Duke of Lancaster, his father). *beg his peace*   from Richard II, who had exiled him.

68. *with cap and knee*   with doffed hat and bended knee; a conventional phrase.

70. *lanes*   lines (making lanes), rather than minor roads, which are unsuited for a triumphal progress.

72. *heirs as pages,*   QqF have *heires, as Pages* but heirs, presumably youthful, would be the pages, not the general populace.

73. *golden*   finely attired.

76. *while . . . poor*   while he lacked pride in rank (and personal confidence).

Some certain edicts, and some strait decrees

80　That lie too heavy on the commonwealth,
Cries out upon abuses, seems to weep
Over his country's wrongs; and by this face,
This seeming brow of justice, did he win
The hearts of all that he did angle for;

85　Proceeded further—cut me off the heads
Of all the favourites that the absent king
In deputation left behind him here,
When he was personal in the Irish war.

BLUNT

Tut, I came not to hear this.

HOTSPUR

　　　　　　　　　Then to the point.

90　In short time after he deposed the king;
Soon after that deprived him of his life,
And in the neck of that tasked the whole state;
To make that worse, suffered his kinsman March
(Who is, if every owner were well placed,

95　Indeed his king) to be engaged in Wales,
There without ransom to lie forfeited;
Disgraced me in my happy victories,
Sought to entrap me by intelligence,
Rated my uncle from the Council-board,

100　In rage dismissed my father from the court;
Broke oath on oath, committed wrong on wrong,
And in conclusion drove us to seek out

---

79. *strait*　strict.
82. *face*　pretense.
83. *brow*　appearance.
87. *In deputation*　as deputies.
88. *personal*　personally engaged.
92. *in the neck of that*　immediately thereafter.
95. *engaged*　held as a hostage (compare V.ii.43).
96. *forfeited*　unredeemed.
98. *intelligence*　spies (compare I.iii.32ff.).
99. *Rated*　berated, scolded.

This head of safety, and withal to pry
Into his title, the which we find
105 Too indirect for long continuance.

BLUNT

Shall I return this answer to the king?

HOTSPUR

Not so, Sir Walter. We'll withdraw awhile.
Go to the king, and let there be impawned
Some surety for a safe return again,
110 And in the morning early shall mine uncle
Bring him our purposes; and so farewell.

BLUNT

I would you would accept of grace and love.

HOTSPUR

And may be so we shall.

BLUNT

Pray God you do.

[Exeunt.]

*[Scene iv: About the same time, at the Archbishop's Palace
in York.] Enter* ARCHBISHOP OF YORK, SIR MICHAEL.

ARCHBISHOP

Hie, good Sir Michael, bear this sealèd brief
With wingèd haste to the lord marshal,
This to my cousin Scroop, and all the rest
To whom they are directed. If you knew

---

103. *head of safety*   army for self-defense.
104. *title*   to the crown.
1. *Sir*   may be used not only for knights, but also priests (as, probably, here). A priest's title, if he held a university B.A. of Oxford, was *dominus*; if of Cambridge, Sir. The character of Sir Michael is invented. *brief*   letter (giving information).
2. *lord marshal*   Thomas Mowbray, Earl of Norfolk, whose rebellion appears in *2HIV*, occupied this position. The word was probably pronounced as a trisyllable, as in French: *maréschal*.

5　How much they do import you would make haste.

SIR MICHAEL

My good lord,
I guess their tenor.

ARCHBISHOP

Like enough you do.
Tomorrow, good Sir Michael, is a day
Wherein the fortune of ten thousand men
10　Must bide the touch. For sir, at Shrewsbury
As I am truly given to understand,
The king with mighty and quick-raisèd power
Meets with Lord Harry. And I fear, Sir Michael—
What with the sickness of Northumberland,
15　Whose power was in the first proportion,
And what with Owen Glendower's absence thence,
Who with them was a rated sinew too,
And comes not in, o'er-ruled by prophecies—
I fear the power of Percy is too weak
20　To wage an instant trial with the king.

SIR MICHAEL

Why, my good lord, you need not fear—
There is Douglas, and Lord Mortimer.

ARCHBISHOP

No, Mortimer is not there.

SIR MICHAEL

But there is Murdoch, Vernon, Lord Harry Percy,
25　And there is my Lord of Worcester, and a head
Of gallant warriors, noble gentlemen.

---

10. *bide the touch*　meet the test (gold was tested by rubbing it on a hard black stone, called a touchstone, and the streak left revealed the quality of the gold to a practiced eye).

15. *in the first proportion*　of the first magnitude.

17. *rated sinew*　highly esteemed support.

18. *comes not*　See IV.i.126, note.

ARCHBISHOP

And so there is; but yet the king hath drawn
The special head of all the land together—
The Prince of Wales, Lord John of Lancaster,
30   The noble Westmoreland, and warlike Blunt,
And many mo corrivals and dear men
Of estimation and command in arms.

SIR MICHAEL

Doubt not, my lord, they shall be well opposed.

ARCHBISHOP

I hope no less, yet needful 'tis to fear;
35   And to prevent the worst, Sir Michael, speed—
For if Lord Percy thrive not, ere the king
Dismiss his power, he means to visit us,
For he hath heard of our confederacy,
And 'tis but wisdom to make strong against him;
40   Therefore make haste. I must go write again
To other friends, and so farewell, Sir Michael.

                                      Exeunt.

[*Act V, scene i: The morning after IV.iii, in the King's camp near Shrewsbury.*] *Enter the* KING, PRINCE OF WALES, LORD JOHN OF LANCASTER, SIR WALTER BLUNT, FALSTAFF.

KING

How bloodily the sun begins to peer
Above yon bulky hill! The day looks pale
At his distemp'rature.

---

31. *mo* more (used of numbers rather than quantity). *corrivals* companions. *dear* noble.

32. *Of estimation* by (qualified) opinion.

35. *prevent* has the sense of "forestall," as well as its modern meaning.

S.D. QqF include Westmoreland among those present, but see V.ii.29*ff*.

2. *bulky* Many editors insist on changing this authentic reading to *busky* (i.e., bosky, wooded), as in *NCS*.

PRINCE

The southern wind

Doth play the trumpet to his purposes,

5   And by his hollow whistling in the leaves

Foretells a tempest and a blust'ring day.

KING

Then with the losers let it sympathize,

For nothing can seem foul to those that win.

The trumpet sounds.

Enter WORCESTER [*and* VERNON].

KING

How now, my Lord of Worcester? 'Tis not well

10   That you and I should meet upon such terms

As now we meet. You have deceived our trust,

And made us doff our easy robes of peace

To crush our old limbs in ungentle steel—

This is not well, my lord, this is not well.

15   What say you to it? Will you again unknit

This churlish knot of all-abhorrèd war,

And move in that obedient orb again

Where you did give a fair and natural light—

And be no more an exhaled meteor,

20   A prodigy of fear, and a portent

Of broachèd mischief to the unborn times?

---

3. *distemp'rature*   disorder.

4. *his purposes*   the sun's plans (for the day's weather).

8. S.D. *and* VERNON   Vernon's presence in this scene is required by his account of it to Hotspur, V.ii.51*ff.*

13. *old*   Henry was now only thirty-six, but Shakespeare stresses, a little prematurely, the marked physical decline of his last years.

16. *knot*   the tangle caused by the rebellion.

17. *obedient orb*   sphere of obedience. Ptolemaic astronomy asserted that stars orbited in strictly defined spheres.

19. *exhaled meteor*   Meteors were supposed to be made of gas given off by some heavenly body, and to be bad omens—compare "portent," and "prodigy of fear" (i.e., provoking fear), line 20.

WORCESTER

Hear me, my liege:
For mine own part I could be well content
To entertain the lag end of my life
25 With quiet hours. For I protest
I have not sought the day of this dislike.

KING

You have not sought it!—how comes it then?

FALSTAFF

Rebellion lay in his way, and he found it.

PRINCE

Peace, chewet, peace!

WORCESTER

30 It pleased your majesty to turn your looks
Of favor from myself, and all our house—
And yet I must remember you, my lord,
We were the first and dearest of your friends;
For you my staff of office did I break
35 In Richard's time, and posted day and night
To meet you on the way, and kiss your hand,
When yet you were in place and in account
Nothing so strong and fortunate as I.
It was myself, my brother, and his son,
40 That brought you home, and boldly did outdare
The dangers of the time. You swore to us,

---

21. *broachèd*   already begun.
25. *I protest*   F lengthens this short line by reading "I do protest."
26. *dislike*   enmity.
29. *chewet*   jackdaw (i.e., chatterer); also, a mince pie—a suitable association for Falstaff.
34. *staff . . . break*   "Worcester, lord steward of the king's [Richard II's] house . . . brake his white staff, which is the representing sign and token of his office, and without delay went to Duke Henry." Holinshed, II,855.
35. *posted*   rode posthaste.
38. *Nothing*   by no means.

And you did swear that oath at Doncaster,
That you did nothing purpose 'gainst the state,
Nor claim no further than your new-fall'n right—
45   The seat of Gaunt, Dukedom of Lancaster.
To this we swore our aid; but in short space
It rained down fortune showering on your head,
And such a flood of greatness fell on you—
What with our help, what with the absent king,
50   What with the injuries of a wanton time,
The seeming sufferances that you had borne,
And the contrarious winds that held the king
So long in his unlucky Irish wars
That all in England did repute him dead—
55   And from this swarm of fair advantages
You took occasion to be quickly wooed
To gripe the general sway into your hand,
Forgot your oath to us at Doncaster,
And, being fed by us, you used us so
60   As that ungentle gull the cuckoo's bird
Useth the sparrow—did oppress our nest,
Grew by our feeding to so great a bulk
That even our love durst not come near your sight
For fear of swallowing; but with a nimble wing
65   We were enforced for safety sake to fly
Out of your sight, and raise this present head—
Whereby we stand opposèd, by such means
As you yourself have forged against yourself
By unkind usage, dangerous countenance,

---

44. *new-fall'n right*   the right newly descended to Henry at the
death of John of Gaunt, his father.

50. *injuries*   troubles. *wanton*   disorderly.

57. *general sway*   rule of the whole kingdom.

60. *gull*   "young, unfledged bird," *OED*; compare "cuckoo's bird"
(i.e., the bird born to the cuckoo).

61. *useth*   The cuckoo lays its eggs in the nests of small birds such
as the sparrow, which the young cuckoo soon exceeds in size.

69. *dangerous countenance*   threatening attitude.

70   And violation of all faith and troth
      Sworn to us in your younger enterprise.

                        KING

      These thing indeed you have articulate,
      Proclaimed at market crosses, read in churches,
      To face the garment of rebellion
75   With some fine colour that may please the eye
      Of fickle changelings and poor discontents,
      Which gape and rub the elbow at the news
      Of hurlyburly innovation;
      And never yet did insurrection want
80   Such water-colours to impaint his cause,
      Nor moody beggars starving for a time
      Of pellmell havoc and confusion.

                        PRINCE

      In both your armies there is many a soul
      Shall pay full dearly for this encounter
85   If once they join in trial. Tell your nephew
      The Prince of Wales doth join with all the world
      In praise of Henry Percy; by my hopes—
      This present enterprise set off his head—
      I do not think a braver gentleman,

---

71. *your younger enterprise*   i.e., your earlier plan.
72. *articulate*   articulated (see p. 169).
74. *face*   trim, make more attractive.
75. *colour*   following the idea of "trim"; but to "colour" was also to excuse.
76. *changelings*   turncoats.
77. *rub the elbow*   hug themselves with delight. Pleasure was supposed to produce itchy elbows; compare *LLL*, V.ii.109–10, "One rubbed his elbow . . . and swore/ A better speech was never heard before."
78. *innovation*   rebellion.
79. *want*   lack.
80. *water-colours*   i.e., easily washed off (compare line 75).
83. *your*   Qq.F reads *our*.
88. *set . . . head*   removed from his account.

90   More active, valiant—or more valiant-young—
      More daring, or more bold, is now alive
      To grace this latter age with noble deeds.
      For my part, I may speak it to my shame,
      I have a truant been to chivalry,
95   And so I hear he doth account me too;
      Yet this, before my father's majesty—
      I am content that he shall take the odds
      Of his great name and estimation,
      And will, to save the blood on either side,
100   Try fortune with him in a single fight.

                           KING

      And, Prince of Wales, so dare we venture thee,
      Albeit considerations infinite
      Do make against it. No, good Worcester, no—
      We love our people well, even those we love
105   That are misled upon your cousin's part,
      And will they take the offer of our grace,
      Both he, and they, and you, yea every man
      Shall be my friend again, and I'll be his;
      So tell your cousin, and bring me word
110   What he will do. But if he will not yield,
      Rebuke and dread Correction wait on us,
      And they shall do their office. So, be gone;
      We will not now be troubled with reply;

---

90. *or . . . young* Hal's diplomatic self-correction recalls the superiority accorded to Douglas (presented in the play as older than Hotspur) at III.ii.107*ff.*, and IV.i.1*ff.* Most editors follow Theobald and merely hyphenate both pairs of adjectives: "Active-valiant or more valiant-young."

100. *single fight* This challenge is Shakespeare's own addition.

102. *Albeit* although.

105. *cousin's part* by joining your nephew's party. "Cousin" was then used more broadly.

111. *wait on us* serve me.

We offer fair—take it advisedly.

Exit WORCESTER [, *with* VERNON].

PRINCE

115 It will not be accepted, on my life—
The Douglas and the Hotspur both together
Are confident against the world in arms.

KING

Hence, therefore, every leader to his charge;
For on their answer will we set on them,
120 And God befriend us, as our cause is just!

Exeunt; PRINCE, FALSTAFF *remain.*

FALSTAFF

Hal, if thou see me down in the battle and bestride me, so, 'tis
a point of friendship.

PRINCE

Nothing but a colossus can do thee that friendship—say thy
prayers, and farewell.

FALSTAFF

125 I would 'twere bed-time, Hal, and all well.

PRINCE

Why, thou owest God a death.

[*Exit.*]

FALSTAFF

'Tis not due yet, I would be loath to pay him before his day—
what need I be so forward with him that calls not on me? Well,
'tis no matter—honour pricks me on; yea, but how if honour
130 prick me off when I come on, how then? Can honour set to a

---

114. *advisedly*   into careful consideration.
119. *on*   on the arrival of.
120. S.D. *remain   manent* Qq. Latin "they remain."
121. *bestride*   i.e., in order to defend me.
126. *thou . . . death*   proverbial (compare *2HIV*, III.ii.229).
129. *pricks*   spurs; contrasted with its sense in the next line—mark
me down (see *JC*, IV.i.1).

leg? No.—or an arm? No.—or take away the grief of a wound?
No. Honour hath no skill in surgery then? No. What is honour? A word. What is in that word honour? What is that honour? Air. A trim reckoning! Who hath it? He that died a-
135   Wednesday. Doth he feel it? No. Doth he hear it? No. 'Tis
insensible, then? Yea, to the dead. But will it not live with the
living? No. Why? Detraction will not suffer it. Therefore I'll
none of it. Honour is a mere scutcheon—and so ends my
catechism.

Exit.

[*Scene ii: A short time thereafter, at the rebel camp near
Shrewsbury.*] *Enter* WORCESTER, SIR RICHARD VERNON.

WORCESTER

O no!—my nephew must not know, Sir Richard,
The liberal and kind offer of the king.

VERNON

'Twere best he did.

WORCESTER

          Then are we all undone.
It is not possible, it cannot be
5   The king should keep his word in loving us;
He will suspect us still, and find a time
To punish this offence in other faults—

134ff. *Who hath it? . . .*   A somewhat similar passage appears in
Palingenius' *Zodiacus Vitae*, used in Elizabethan schools (see T. W.
Baldwin, *William Shakespeare's Small Latin and Less Greek* [Urbana,
1944] I, 678)—Falstaff's manner suggests that of a schoolboy being
questioned. Montaigne's essay "Of Glory" may have suggested Falstaff's ideas also.

136. *insensible*   imperceptible.

138. *scutcheon*   an heraldic design of a temporary kind, used for
funerals, or on tombs, etc.

3. *all undone*   Q5,F. Qq1–4 read *under one.*

6. *still*   always.

Supposition all our lives shall be stuck full of eyes,
For Treason is but trusted like the fox,
10   Who, ne'er so tame, so cherished and locked up,
Will have a wild trick of his ancestors.
Look how we can, or sad or merrily,
Interpretation will misquote our looks,
And we shall feed like oxen at a stall—
15   The better cherished still the nearer death.
My nephew's trespass may be well forgot,
It hath the excuse of youth and heat of blood,
And an adopted name of privilege—
A hare-brained "Hotspur," governed by a spleen:
20   All his offences live upon my head
And on his father's. We did train him on,
And his corruption being ta'en from us,
We as the spring of all shall pay for all;
Therefore, good cousin, let not Harry know
25   In any case the offer of the king.

VERNON

Deliver what you will, I'll say 'tis so.
Here comes your cousin.

Enter HOTSPUR [*and* DOUGLAS].

HOTSPUR
My uncle is returned;

---

8. *Supposition*   QqF. Most editors insist on "improving" this line
by changing this word to *Suspicion*.

10. *ne'er so tame*   no matter how tame.

11. *trick*   trait.

12. *sad*   serious.

18. *adopted . . . privilege*   a nickname (Hotspur) that seems to au-
thorize rashness.

19. *hare . . . spleen*   See note to II.iii.72.

20. *live . . . head*   are my responsibility.

27. S.D. *Enter* HOTSPUR   F. Q1 has *Enter* PERCY (after line 25). Qq2–
5 have *Enter* HOTSPUR (after line 25).

Deliver up my Lord of Westmoreland.
Uncle, what news?

WORCESTER

30 The king will bid you battle presently.

DOUGLAS

Defy him by the Lord of Westmoreland.

HOTSPUR

Lord Douglas, go you and tell him so.

DOUGLAS

Marry, and shall, and very willingly.

Exit [DOUGLAS.]

WORCESTER

There is no seeming mercy in the king.

HOTSPUR

35 Did you beg any? God forbid!

WORCESTER

I told him gently of our grievances,
Of his oath-breaking—which he mended thus,
By now forswearing that he is forsworn;
He calls us rebels, traitors, and will scourge
40 With haughty arms this hateful name in us.

[*Re-*]*enter* DOUGLAS.

DOUGLAS

Arm, gentlemen! To arms!—for I have thrown
A brave defiance in King Henry's teeth,
And Westmoreland that was engaged did bear it,
Which cannot choose but bring him quickly on.

---

30. *presently*   at once.
34. *seeming*   appearance of.
38. *forswearing*   taking a false oath.
40. *this . . . us*   this evil character of rebels which we have acquired.
43. *engaged*   held hostage.

WORCESTER

45 The Prince of Wales stepped forth before the king
And, nephew, challenged you to single fight.

HOTSPUR

O, would the quarrel lay upon our heads,
And that no man might draw short breath today
But I and Harry Monmouth! Tell me, tell me
50 How he showed his tasking?—seemed it in contempt?

VERNON

No, by my soul, I never in my life
Did hear a challenge urged more modestly,
Unless a brother should a brother dare
To gentle exercise and proof of arms.
55 He gave you all the duties of a man,
Trimmed up your praises with a princely tongue,
Spoke your deservings like a chronicle,
Making you ever better than his praise
By still dispraising praise valued with you;
60 And, which became him like a prince indeed,
He made a blushing cital of himself,
And chid his truant youth with such a grace
As if he mastered there a double spirit
Of teaching and of learning instantly.
65 There he did pause; but let me tell the world,
If he outlive the envy of this day,
England did never owe so sweet a hope,
So much misconstrued in his wantonness.

---

50. *tasking* making challenge (compare "take to task").
55. *duties of a man* the courtesies due one man from another.
56. *trimmed up* adorned, heightened.
59. *valued with you* compared to your actual (indescribable) value.
61. *cital* either *recital* (account), or *accusation* (compare *citation*).
64. *instantly* at the same instant.
66. *envy* hostility.
67. *owe* own.

HOTSPUR

Cousin, I think thou art enamourèd
70 On his follies—never did I hear
Of any prince so wild a liberty;
But be he as he will, yet once ere night
I will embrace him with a soldier's arm,
That he shall shrink under my courtesy.
75 Arm, arm with speed!—and fellows, soldiers, friends,
Better consider what you have to do
Than I that have not well the gift of tongue
Can lift your blood up with persuasion.

Enter a Messenger.

MESSENGER

My lord, here are letters for you.

HOTSPUR

80 I cannot read them now.
O gentlemen, the time of life is short!—
To spend that shortness basely were too long
If life did ride upon a dial's point,
Still ending at the arrival of an hour.
85 And if we live, we live to tread on kings,
If die, brave death when princes die with us!
Now, for our consciences—the arms are fair
When the intent of bearing them is just . . .

Enter another [Messenger].

MESSENGER

My lord, prepare—the king comes on apace.

HOTSPUR

90 I thank him that he cuts me from my tale,
For I profess not talking; only this—
Let each man do his best, and here draw I

---

71. *liberty*   lack of restraint: "Liberty plucks Justice by the nose,"
Measure, I.iii.29.
83–4. *if . . . hour*   i.e., even if life lasted only an hour.

A sword whose temper I intend to stain
With the best blood that I can meet withal
95 In the adventure of this perilous day.
Now—"Esperance! Percy!"—and set on!
Sound all the lofty instruments of war,
And by that music let us all embrace,
For, heaven to earth, some of us never shall
100 A second time do such a courtesy.

> *Here they embrace, the trumpets sound, [exeunt].*

[Scene iii: Shortly thereafter, on the field of battle near Shrewsbury.] The KING *enters with his power; alarum to battle [and they leave].*
Then enter DOUGLAS *and* SIR WALTER BLUNT *[disguised as the King].*

BLUNT

What is thy name that in the battle thus
Thou crossest me? What honour dost thou seek
Upon my head?

DOUGLAS

        Know then my name is Douglas,
And I do haunt thee in the battle thus
5 Because some tell me that thou art a king.

BLUNT

They tell thee true.

DOUGLAS

The Lord of Stafford dear today hath bought
Thy likeness, for instead of thee, King Harry,

---

96. *"Esperance! Percy"*   Battle cries; see II.iii.65. Perhaps the final "e" of "Esperance" is voiced, as in French pronunciation.

99. *heaven to earth*   by odds of infinite to finite.

S.D. These appear in QqF without a break after those now printed at the end of V.ii.

1. *in the battle*   in battle QqF (but see line 4, which suggests how to correct the short line).

10   This sword hath ended him—so shall it thee
      Unless thou yield thee as my prisoner.

                          BLUNT

      I was not born a yielder, thou proud Scot,
      And thou shalt find a king that will revenge
      Lord Stafford's death.

                          They fight. DOUGLAS *kills* BLUNT.

                   Then enter HOTSPUR.

                          HOTSPUR

      O Douglas, hadst thou fought at Holmedon thus
15   I never had triumphed upon a Scot.

                          DOUGLAS

      All's done, all's won—here breathless lies the king.

                          HOTSPUR

      Where?

                          DOUGLAS

      Here.

                          HOTSPUR

      This, Douglas? No, I know this face full well;
20   A gallant knight he was, his name was Blunt—
      Semblably furnished like the king himself.

                          DOUGLAS

      "A fool" go with thy soul, whither it goes!
      A borrowed title hast thou bought too dear.
      Why didst thou tell me that thou wert a king?

                          HOTSPUR

25   The king hath many marching in his coats.

---

21. *semblably furnished*   equipped to seem like.
22. *"A fool" go*   i.e., as description. Qq read: *Ah foole, goe. . . .*
Capell suggested the emendation. (Compare Whetstone, *Promos and Cassandra*, 1578, II.iv.15: "Go and a knave with thee.")
25. *coats*   the outer coat bearing heraldic crests, worn over armor for identification.

DOUGLAS

Now, by my sword, I will kill all his coats.
I'll murder all his wardrobe piece by piece
Until I meet the king.

HOTSPUR

Up and away!
Our soldiers stand full fairly for the day.

[*Exeunt.*]

Alarum. Enter FALSTAFF *solus.*

FALSTAFF

30   Though I could scape shot-free at London, I fear the shot here
—here's no scoring but upon the pate. Soft!—who are you? Sir
Walter Blunt?—there's honour for you! Here's no vanity! I am
as hot as molten lead, and as heavy too; God keep lead out of
me, I need no more weight than mine own bowels. I have led
35   my ragamuffins where they are peppered—there's not three of
my hundred and fifty left alive, and they are for the town's
end, to beg during life. But who comes here?

Enter the PRINCE.

PRINCE

What, stands thou idle here? Lend me thy sword—
Many a nobleman lies stark and stiff

---

29. *fairly for the day*   strongly enough to win the day's fighting.

30. *shot*   reckoning (at taverns)—with a pun on the military meaning.

31. *scoring*   i.e., both: marking a reckoning, and gouging. *Soft!*
Wait a moment!

32. *no vanity*   no mere deceptive show (of honor).

34. *led*   Editors like A. R. Humphreys have tried to demonstrate
that this word cannot be taken literally, but this remains an interpretation, not self-evident. Dead soldiers' pay could easily be illegally collected by cowardly captains, and this *might* be Falstaff's plan (as in Sir
John Smythe, *Certain Discourses Military*, 1590, sig.3).

36–7. *town's end*   where beggars would wait for alms from travelers.

38. *stands*   For ease of pronunciation verbs ending in 't' and 'd'
often took this form of second person singular (compare line 48).

40   Under the hoofs of vaunting enemies,
Whose deaths are yet unrevenged—I prithee
Lend me thy sword.

FALSTAFF

O Hal, I prithee give me leave to breathe awhile—Turk
Gregory never did such deeds in arms as I have done this day:
45   I have paid Percy, I have made him sure.

PRINCE

He is indeed, and living to kill thee;
I prithee lend me thy sword.

FALSTAFF

Nay, before God, Hal, if Percy be alive thou gets not my sword,
but take my pistol if you wilt.

PRINCE

50   Give it me; what, is it in the case?

FALSTAFF

Ay, Hal, 'tis hot, 'tis hot; there's that will sack a city.
The PRINCE *draws it out, and finds it to be a bottle of sack.*

PRINCE

What, is it a time to jest and dally now?
                     He throws the bottle at him. Exit.

FALSTAFF

Well, if Percy be alive, I'll pierce him. If he do come in my way,

---

43–4. *Turk Gregory* "Turkish" was synonymous with fierceness. There were two Popes called Gregory whose fierceness drew Protestant censure—the second, Shakespeare's contemporary Gregory XIII, ruled 1572–1585, and approved of the St. Bartholemew massacre of Huguenots. Gregory VII, 1073–85 (previously known as Hildebrand), humiliated Emperor Henry IV at Canossa (but is the less likely allusion despite the anachronism of the alternative, according to *NCS*).
45. *paid* settled the account with (i.e., killed). *sure* safe.
48. *gets* See line 38.
53. *pierce* a pun on Percy?

so; if he do not, if I come in his willingly, let him make a car-
55   bonado of me. I like not such grinning honour as Sir Walter
hath—give me life, which if I can save, so; if not, honour comes
unlooked for, and there's an end.

[*Exit.*]

[*Scene iv: The same.*] *Alarum, excursions. Enter the* KING,
the PRINCE, LORD JOHN OF LANCASTER, EARL OF WESTMORELAND.

KING

I prithee, Harry, withdraw thyself; thou bleedest too much.
Lord John of Lancaster, go you with him.

JOHN

Not I, my lord, unless I did bleed too.

PRINCE

I beseech your majesty—make up,
5   Lest your retirement do amaze your friends.

KING

I will do so. My Lord of Westmoreland,
Lead him to his tent.

WESTMORELAND

Come, my lord, I'll lead you to your tent.

PRINCE

Lead me, my lord? I do not need your help,
10   And God forbid a shallow scratch should drive
The Prince of Wales from such a field as this,
Where stained nobility lies trodden on,
And rebels' arms triumph in massacres.

JOHN

We breathe too long; come, cousin Westmoreland,

54–5. *carbonado*   barbecued meat.
4. *make up*   advance.
5. *amaze*   disconcert.
14. *breathe*   pause for breath.

15   Our duty this way lies—for God's sake come!

[*Exit* JOHN, *with* WESTMORELAND.]

PRINCE

By God, thou hast deceived me, Lancaster,
I did not think thee lord of such a spirit;
Before, I loved thee as a brother, John,
But now I do respect thee as my soul.

KING

20   I saw him hold Lord Percy at the point
With lustier maintenance than I did look for
Of such an ungrown warrior.

PRINCE

O this boy

Lends mettle to us all!

Exit.

[*Enter* DOUGLAS.]

DOUGLAS

Another king!—they grow like Hydra's heads.
25   I am the Douglas, fatal to all those
That wear those colours on them. What art thou
That counterfeit'st the person of a king?

KING

The king himself who, Douglas, grieves at heart
So many of his shadows thou hast met,
30   And not the very king. I have two boys
Seek Percy and thyself about the field,
But seeing thou fall'st on me so luckily
I will assay thee; and defend thyself.

---

20. *point*   sword's point.
24. *Hydra's heads*   As each of the monster Hydra's many heads
was cut off, two new ones sprouted, according to Greek mythology.
(Hercules finally killed it, by cauterizing the wounds.)
26. *those colours*   the King's coat of arms.

DOUGLAS

I fear thou art another counterfeit,
35   And yet, in faith, thou bearest thee like a king;
But mine I am sure thou art, whoe'er thou be,
And thus I win thee.

> *They fight, the* KING *being in danger.*

[Re-]enter PRINCE OF WALES.

PRINCE

Hold up thy head, vile Scot, or thou art like
Never to hold it up again!—the spirits
40   Of valiant Shirley, Stafford, Blunt are in my arms;
It is the Prince of Wales that threatens thee,
Who never promiseth but he means to pay.

> *They fight;* DOUGLAS *flieth.*

Cheerly, my lord—how fares your grace?
Sir Nicholas Gawsey hath for succour sent,
45   And so hath Clifton—I'll to Clifton straight.

KING

Stay and breathe awhile . . .
Thou hast redeemed thy lost opinion,
And showed thou mak'st some tender of my life
In this fair rescue thou hast brought to me.

PRINCE

50   O God, they did me too much injury
That ever said I hearkened for your death;
If it were so, I might have let alone
The insulting hand of Douglas over you—
Which would have been as speedy in your end
55   As all the poisonous potions in the world,
And saved the treacherous labour of your son.

---

47. *opinion* reputation.
48. *mak'st some tender of* have some regard for.
53. *insulting* by its triumph.

KING

Make up to Clifton; I'll to Sir Nicholas Gawsey.

Exit [KING.]

Enter HOTSPUR.

HOTSPUR

If I mistake not, thou art Harry Monmouth.

PRINCE

Thou speak'st as if I would deny my name.

HOTSPUR

My name is Harry Percy!

PRINCE

60   Why then I see
A very valiant rebel of the name.
I am the Prince of Wales, and think not Percy
To share with me in glory any more:
Two stars keep not their motion in one sphere,
65   Nor can one England brook a double reign
Of Harry Percy and the Prince of Wales.

HOTSPUR

Nor shall it, Harry, for the hour is come
To end the one of us, and would to God
Thy name in arms were now as great as mine.

PRINCE

70   I'll make it greater ere I part from thee,
And all the budding honours on thy crest
I'll crop to make a garland for my head.

HOTSPUR

I can no longer brook thy vanities.

They fight.

---

57. *Make up to* give support to (by joining; compare line 4).

64. *Two . . . sphere* Ptolemaic astronomy maintained that each star had its own fixed sphere.

67. *Nor* F. Qq read *Now*.

Enter FALSTAFF.

FALSTAFF

Well said, Hal!—to it Hal! Nay, you shall find no boy's play
75　here, I can tell you.

Enter DOUGLAS: *he fighteth with* FALSTAFF, [*who*]
falls down as if he were dead. [*Exit* DOUGLAS.]
The PRINCE *killeth* HOTSPUR:

HOTSPUR

O Harry, thou hast robbed me of my youth.
I better brook the loss of brittle life
Than those proud titles thou hast won of me;
They wound my thoughts worse than thy sword my flesh;
80　But thoughts (the slaves of Life), and Life (Time's fool),
And Time (that takes survey of all the world),
Must have a stop. O, I could prophesy,
But that the earthy and cold hand of death
Lies on my tongue; no, Percy, thou art dust
85　And food for . . .

　　　　　　　　　　　　　　　　　　　　[*He dies.*]

PRINCE

For worms, brave Percy. Fare thee well, great heart!
Ill-weaved ambition, how much art thou shrunk!
When that this body did contain a spirit
A kingdom for it was too small a bound,
90　But now two paces of the vilest earth

---

74. *Well said*   Well done (a colloquialism; compare *Titus*, IV.iii.63:
"*Titus*: Now, masters draw. [*They shoot.*] O, well said, Lucius").

75. *S.D.* HOTSPUR   PERCY QqF.

80. *thoughts (the slaves* Q1 (less parentheses). Q2–5,F have
thought's the slave; this reading (as in *NCS*) makes "Time," line 81,
the sole subject of "must have a stop," line 82. The parentheses in
lines 80–81 are mine. The Q1 reading matches line 79: "thoughts."

82. *prophesy*   It was believed that dying men could foretell the
future (compare the dying Gaunt: "Methinks I am a prophet new in-
spired," *RII*, II.i.31).

87. *Ill . . . shrunk*   Badly made cloth shrinks.

Is room enough. This earth that bears thee dead
Bears not alive so stout a gentleman.
If thou wert sensible of courtesy
I should not make so dear a show of zeal—
95   But let my favours hide thy mangled face,
And even in thy behalf I'll thank myself
For doing these fair rites of tenderness.
Adieu, and take thy praise with thee to heaven;
Thy ignominy sleep with thee in the grave,
100   But not remembered in thy epitaph.

He spieth FALSTAFF [*lying*] *on the ground.*

What, old acquaintance, could not all this flesh
Keep in a little life? Poor Jack, farewell!
I could have better spared a better man;
O, I should have a heavy miss of thee,
105   If I were much in love with vanity:
Death hath not struck so fat a deer today,
Though many dearer, in this bloody fray.
Embowelled will I see thee by and by,
Till then in blood by noble Percy lie.

Exit.

FALSTAFF *riseth up.*

FALSTAFF

110   Embowelled!—if thou embowel me today, I'll give you leave
to powder me and eat me too tomorrow. 'Sblood, 'twas time

---

94. *dear*   heartfelt.
95. *favours*   strip of cloth worn for identification, or in honor of
the giver (often as a lady's sign of preference—hence, "favour").
104. *heavy . . . thee*   regret thy loss profoundly (with a play on
"heavy").
108. *Embowelled*   disembowelled (for embalming).
111. *powder me*   pickle me with salt.

to counterfeit, or that hot termagant Scot had paid me scot and
lot too. Counterfeit?—I lie, I am no counterfeit, to die is to be
a counterfeit, for he is but the counterfeit of a man, who hath
115   not the life of a man; but to counterfeit dying when a man
thereby liveth is to be no counterfeit, but the true and perfect
image of life indeed. The better part of valour is discretion, in
the which better part I have saved my life. 'Zounds, I am afraid
of this gunpowder Percy, though he be dead—how if he should
120   counterfeit too and rise? By my faith, I am afraid he would
prove the better counterfeit; therefore I'll make him sure—
yea, and I'll swear I killed him. Why may not he rise as well
as I? Nothing confutes me but eyes, and nobody sees me;
therefore, sirrah—with a new wound in your thigh—come you
125   along with me.

He takes up HOTSPUR *on his back.*

Enter PRINCE [OF WALES], JOHN OF LANCASTER.

PRINCE

Come, brother John, full bravely hast thou fleshed
Thy maiden sword.

JOHN

                    But soft, whom have we here?
Did you not tell me this fat man was dead?

PRINCE

I did; I saw him dead—
130   Breathless and bleeding on the ground. Art thou alive?
Or is it fantasy that plays upon our eyesight?

112–13. *termagant*   violent; from Tervagant, a supposed Moham-
medan demon. *scot and lot*   an old form of property tax; Falstaff uses
it to imply "paid in full."
117. *part*   quality. The maxim meant that valour should be governed by good judgment if it is not to be held rashness (compare Hotspur); but Falstaff distorts its bearing.
123. *Nothing . . . eyes*   Only a witness will be able to refute my
account.

I prithee speak; we will not trust our eyes
Without our ears—thou art not what thou seem'st!

FALSTAFF

No, that's certain—I am not a double-man; but if I be not
135   Jack Falstaff, then am I a Jack. There is Percy; if your father
will do me any honour, so; if not, let him kill the next Percy
himself. I look to be either earl or duke, I can assure you.

PRINCE

Why, Percy I killed myself, and saw thee dead.

FALSTAFF

Didst thou? Lord, Lord, how this world is given to lying—I
140   grant you I was down and out of breath, and so was he; but
we rose both at an instant, and fought a long hour by Shrewsbury clock. If I may be believed, so; if not, let them that should
reward valour bear the sin upon their own heads. I'll take it
upon my death, I gave him this wound in the thigh; if the man
145   were alive, and would deny it, 'zounds, I would make him eat
a piece of my sword.

JOHN

This is the strangest tale that ever I heard.

PRINCE

This is the strangest fellow, brother John.
Come, bring your luggage nobly on your back.
150   For my part, if a lie may do thee grace,
I'll gild it with the happiest terms I have.

A retreat is sounded.

The trumpet sounds retreat—the day is ours.
Come, brother, let us to the highest of the field,

---

134. *double-man* ghost (compare *doppelgänger*). Falstaff also
plays on the fact that he is big enough for two men, or that he is carrying Hotspur's body.

135. *Jack* rascal.

143–4. *take . . . death* swear, under penalty of death for falsehood.

150–51. Probably an aside to Falstaff alone.

To see what friends are living, who are dead.

                Exeunt [the PRINCE *and* JOHN OF LANCASTER*].*

FALSTAFF

155   I'll follow, as they say, for reward. He that rewards me, God reward him! If I do grow great, I'll grow less—for I'll purge, and
leave sack, and live cleanly as a nobleman should do.

                        Exit [with the body].

[Scene v: The Same.] The trumpets sound. Enter the KING,
PRINCE OF WALES, LORD JOHN OF LANCASTER, EARL OF WESTMORE-
LAND, *with* WORCESTER *and* VERNON *prisoners.*

KING

Thus ever did rebellion find rebuke.
Ill-spirited Worcester, did not we send grace,
Pardon, and terms of love to all of you?
And wouldst thou turn our offers contrary?—
5   Misuse the tenor of thy kinsman's trust?
Three knights upon our party slain today,
A noble earl and many a creature else
Had been alive this hour,
If like a Christian thou hadst truly borne
10   Betwixt our armies true intelligence.

WORCESTER

What I have done my safety urged me to;
And I embrace this fortune patiently,
Since not to be avoided it falls on me.

---

155. *as they say* "follow" is used of servants' employment for
money; the expression may also apply to hounds who follow game,
and are rewarded by parts of the quarry (here, Hotspur's reputation,
perhaps).

156. *purge* reform.

5. *tenor . . . trust* substance of the duty laid on you by Hotspur.

6. *Three* Holinshed mentions ten.

10. *intelligence* information.

KING

Bear Worcester to the death and Vernon too;

15   Other offenders we will pause upon.

        [WORCESTER *and* VERNON *are taken away under guard.*]

How goes the field?

PRINCE

The noble Scot, Lord Douglas, when he saw

The fortune of the day quite turned from him,

The noble Percy slain and all his men

20   Upon the foot of fear, fled with the rest

And, falling from a hill, he was so bruised

That the pursuers took him. At my tent

The Douglas is, and I beseech your grace

I may dispose of him.

KING

        With all my heart.

PRINCE

25   Then, brother John of Lancaster, to you

This honorable bounty shall belong—

Go to the Douglas and deliver him

Up to his pleasure, ransomless and free;

His valours shown upon our crests today

30   Have taught us how to cherish such high deeds,

Even in the bosom of our adversaries.

JOHN

I thank your grace for this high courtesy,

Which I shall give away immediately.

KING

Then this remains, that we divide our power:

35   You, son John, and my cousin Westmoreland,

---

20. *Upon . . . fear*   i.e., fleeing in fear.

26. *bounty*   generosity.

33. *give away*   pass on.

32–3. Qq1–4. Omitted in Q5,F.

Towards York shall bend you with your dearest speed
To meet Northumberland and the prelate Scroop,
Who, as we hear, are busily in arms;
Myself and you, son Harry, will towards Wales,
40　To fight with Glendower and the Earl of March.
Rebellion in this land shall lose his sway,
Meeting the check of such another day,
And since this business so fair is done,
Let us not leave till all our own be won.

　　　　　　　　　　　　　　　　　Exeunt.

---

36. *dearest*　most zealous.
43. *business*　pronounced with three syllables.

APPENDIX A
A Shakespeare Chronology

1557 (about). John Shakespeare of Stratford-on-Avon marries Mary Arden (they are to have four daughters, all but one of whom dies young, and three sons including William).

1558 November 17. Queen Elizabeth accedes to the throne.

1564 April 26. William Shakespeare, eldest son and third child of John and Mary Shakespeare, christened.

1568 September 4. John Shakespeare becomes bailiff, the most important official in Stratford's administration.

1582 November 27. The license for Shakespeare's marriage to Anne Hathaway of Stratford is issued by the bishop's office in Worcester. The bishop's register, probably mistakenly, calls his wife Anne Whately of Temple Grafton. The marriage may have been effectively contracted earlier.

1583 May 26. Shakespeare's first child, Susanna, is christened at Stratford.

1585 February 2. Twins, Hamnet and Judith Shakespeare, are christened at Stratford.

1585–1591 No references have been found to this period of Shakespeare's life.

1588 Philip II of Spain attempts to reconquer England for Catholicism with the Armada, which is defeated by storms and the English fleet.

1591–1592 Christopher Marlowe writes *Edward II*, model for Shakespeare's *Richard II* (of which *Henry IV, Part 1*, is a continuation).

1592 First recorded production of a play written (or at least revised) by Shakespeare: *Henry VI, Part 1*. Robert Greene attacks his rival and successor, Shakespeare, in *A Groatsworth of Wit*.

1593 Shakespeare dedicates his long poem, *Venus and Adonis*, to the young Earl of Southampton (to whom also, in 1594, he will dedicate his next poem, *The Rape of Lucrece*).

1594 After a period of disorder caused by the plague and frequent bankruptcies among dramatic companies, two groups of players survive: the Lord Admiral's Men, run by sharers including Philip Henslowe the financier and his actor son-in-law Edward Alleyn; and the Lord Chamberlain's Men, run by sharers including Shakespeare and the actor Richard Burbage.

1596 August 11. Hamnet, Shakespeare's only son, buried in Stratford.

1596 October 20. The College of Heralds grants the arms of a gentleman to John Shakespeare (probably at his son's instigation, as John is no longer prospering).

1596 or 1597. First production of *Henry IV, Part 1*; later revised and printed in 1598.

1597 May 4. Shakespeare pays a fee to buy New Place, a large house in Stratford.

1598 Francis Meres writes in his book *Palladis Tamia*: "As Plautus and Seneca are accounted the best for comedy and tragedy among the Latins, so Shakespeare among the English is the most excellent in both kinds for the stage: for comedy, witness his *Gentlemen of Verona*, his *Errors*, his *Love's Labour's Lost*, his *Love's Labour's Won* [= *The Taming of the Shrew*?], his *Midsummer-Night's Dream*, and his *Merchant of Venice*; for tragedy, his *Richard II, Richard III, Henry IV, King John, Titus Andronicus*, and his *Romeo and Juliet*." The list omits the three parts of *Henry VI*.

1599 Opening of the Globe theater, specially built by Shakespeare's company, the Lord Chamberlain's Men.

1600 (about). Shakespeare's version of *Hamlet* first performed. In the next few years he will write the other major tragedies *Othello, Macbeth,* and *King Lear*.

1601 February 8. Robert, Earl of Essex, friend of Shakespeare and possible model for some of his characters (e.g., Hotspur), leads a revolt against Queen Elizabeth; he is executed on February 25. To emphasize a precedent for attempting to depose Elizabeth, he paid Shakespeare's company to perform *Richard II* before the rebellion.

1601 September 8. Shakespeare's father, John, is buried.

1603 March 24. Queen Elizabeth dies. James I (already James VI, King of Scotland) succeeds her. Shakespeare's company becomes the King's Men, and officers of the royal household.

1608–1609 Shakespeare's company acquires a roofed theater, the Blackfriars. He begins to write romances: *Pericles, Cymbeline, The Winter's Tale,* and *The Tempest*.

1610 (about). Shakespeare moves permanently back to Stratford from London.

1613 June 29. The Globe Theater burns down during a performance of what is probably the last play to which Shakespeare contributed, *Henry VIII*.

1616 April 23. Shakespeare dies; according to legend, from a chill contracted at a reunion drinking party with his old friends and fellow authors Ben Jonson and Michael Drayton.

1623 November 8. The First Folio edition of Shakespeare's collected works (gathered by fellow actors Heminges and Condell) is registered for publication at the Stationers' Company, and is published late in the year.

1670 February 17. Shakespeare's granddaughter and last direct descendant, Elizabeth Bernard, is buried.

APPENDIX B
Sources for Henry IV, Part 1

Henry IV, Part 1, has numerous sources (some, like Nashe's *Unfortunate Traveller* and Spenser's *Faerie Queene*, usually provide only imagery, as in IV.i.98–9—see note—and A. R. Humphreys' edition, pp. 201–2), but the writings from which Shakespeare drew the major outlines of his play may be reduced to three (for some others, see the Introduction, pp. xx–xxii).

The basic historical outlines of the plot depend heavily on Raphael Holinshed's *The Chronicles of England, Scotland, and Ireland* (second edition, 1587). The following extracts, taken from the six-volume reprint of 1807–8, will give some sense of the relationship of this work to the text of *Henry IV, Part 1*. Although these extracts provide the closest analogies to the play (of which the parallels are noted parenthetically after each extract), only about a quarter of the relevant parts of Holinshed are cited.

Almost all the material about the course of the Percys' rebellion appears in Holinshed (though often Holinshed gives no precedents for some of the personal relationships involved, such as Hotspur's exchanges with his wife and his quarrel with Glendower). The failure of Mortimer's expedition against the Welsh and "the shamefull villainy used by the Welshwomen towards the dead" (compare I.i.36–46) are followed in Holinshed by an account of Henry IV's reaction to the capture of Mortimer (all the following extracts about the Percys appear in Volume III of the 1807–8 edition, pages 20–27):

"The king was not hasty to purchase the deliverance of the Earl March, because his title to the crown was well enough known, and therefore suffered him to remain in miserable prison, wishing both the said earl, and all other of his lineage out of this life, with God and his saints in heaven, so they had been out of the way. . . ." [Compare I.iii. 88–91; also the imagery at III.i.8–12.]

The failure of Henry IV's expeditions and the magical sources of these defeats are explained in Holinshed's account of one of them:

"About mid of August, the king to chastise the presumptuous attempts of the Welshmen, went with a great power of men into Wales, to pursue the captain of the Welsh rebel, Owen Glendower, but in effect he lost his labor; for Owen conveyed himself out of the way, into his known lurking places, and (as was thought) through art magic, he caused such foul weather of winds, tempest, rain, snow, and hail to be raised, for the annoyance of the king's army, that the like had not been heard of; in such sort, that the king was constrained to return home. . . [Compare III.i.42–66.] Strange wonders happened (as men reported) at the nativity of this man . . ." [i.e., Glendower]. [Compare III.i.12–41.]

The origins of the Percys' revolt are described as follows:

"Henry Earl of Northumberland, with his brother Thomas Earl of Worcester, and his son the Lord Henry Percy, surnamed Hotspur, which were to King Henry in the beginning of his reign, both faithfull friends, and earnest aiders, began now to envy his wealth and felicity; and especially they were grieved, because the king demanded of the earl and his son such Scottish prisoners as were taken at Homeldon and Nesbit: for of all the captives which were taken in the conflicts foughten in those two places, there was delivered to the king's possession only Murdoch, Earl of Fife, the Duke of Albany's son, though the king did diverse and sundry times require deliverance of the residue, and with great threatenings [compare I.i.92ff.]: wherewith the Percys being sore offended, for that they claimed them as their own proper prisoners, and their peculiar preys, by the counsel of the Lord Thomas Percy Earl of Worcester, whose study was ever (as some write) to procure malice, and set things in a broil, came to the king unto Windsor (upon a purpose to prove him) and there required of him, that either by ransom or otherwise, he would cause to be delivered out of prison Edmund Mortimer Earl of March, their cousin germane, whom (as they reported) Owen Glendower kept in filthy prison, shackled with irons, only for that he took his part, and was to him faithful and true.

"The king began not a little to muse at this request, and not without cause: for indeed it touched him somewhat near, sith this Edmund was son to Roger Earl of March, son to the Lady Philip, daughter of Lionel Duke of Clarence, the third son of King Edward the Third; which Edmund at King Richard's going into Ireland, was proclaimed heir apparent to the crown and realm, whose aunt called Elianor [actually Elizabeth], the Lord Henry Percy had married; and therefore King Henry could not well hear, that any man should be earnest about the advancement of that lineage. The king when he had studied on the matter, made answer, that the Earl of March was not taken prisoner for his cause nor in his service, but willingly suffered himself to be taken, because he would not withstand the attempts of Owen Glendower, and his complices, and therefore he would neither ransom him, nor relieve him.

"The Percys with this answer and fraudulent excuse were not a little fumed, insomuch that Henry Hotspur said openly: 'Behold, the heir of the realm is robbed of his right, and yet the robber with his own will not redeem him.' So in this fury the Percys departed, minding nothing more than to depose King Henry from the high type of his royalty, and to place in his seat their cousin, Edmund Earl of March, whom they did not only deliver out of captivity, but also (to the high displeasure of King Henry) entered in league with the foresaid Owen Glendower." [Compare I.iii, throughout.]

The description of the battle of Shrewsbury affords some close analogies between Holinshed and Shakespeare (much of the intermediate historical detail also comes from Holinshed):

"The next day in the morning early, being the even of Mary Magdalene, they set their battles in order on both sides, and now whilst the warriors looked when the token of battle should be given, the abbot of Shrewsbury, and one of the Clerks of the Privy Seal, were sent from the king into the Percys, to offer them pardon, if they would come to any reasonable agreement. By their persuasions, the Lord Henry Percy began to give ear unto the king's offers, and so sent with them his uncle the Earl of Worcester, to declare unto the king the causes of those troubles, and to require some effectual reformation of the same.

"It was reported for a truth, that now when the king had condescended unto all that was reasonable at his hands to be required, and seemed to humble himself more than was meet for his estate, the Earl of Worcester (upon his return to his nephew) made relation clean contrary to that the king had said, in such sort that he set his nephew's heart more in displeasure towards the king, then ever it was before, driving him by that means to fight whether he would or not: then suddenly blew the trumpets, the king's part crying 'Saint George' upon them, the adversaries cried 'Esperance Percy', and so the two armies furiously joined. . . ." [Compare IV.iii–V.ii.]

"The Prince that day holp his father like a lusty young gentleman: for although he was hurt in the face with an arrow, so that diverse noble men that were about him, would have conveyed him forth of the field, yet he would not suffer them so to do, lest his departure from amongst his men might happily have striken some fear into their hearts. . . . at length, the king crying 'Saint George, victory,' brake the array of his enemies, and adventured so far, that (as some write) the Earl Douglas strake him down, and at that instant slew Sir Walter Blunt, and three other, apparelled in the king's suit and clothing, saying: 'I marvel to see so many kings thus suddenly arise one in the neck of an other.' The king indeed was raised, and did that day many a noble feat of arms, for as it is written, he slew that day with his own hands six and thirty persons of his enemies. The other on his part encouraged by his doings, fought valiantly, and slew the Lord Percy, called Sir Henry Hotspur. To conclude, the king's enemies were vanquished, and put to flight, in which flight, the Earl of Douglas, for haste, falling from the crag of an high mountain, brake one of his cullions, and was taken, and for his valiantness, of the king frankly and freely delivered." [Compare V.iii–v.]

These passages about the Percy rebellion were certainly reinforced
by Samuel Daniel's account in *The First Four Books of the Civil Wars
Between the Two Houses of Lancaster and York* (1595). In Book III
Daniel gives this account of the start of the rebellion (stanzas 86–89,
91):

> And yet new Hydras lo, new heads appear
> T'afflict that peace reputed then so sure,
> And gave him much to do, and much to fear,
> And long and dangerous tumults did procure,
> And those even of his chiefest followers were
> Of whom he might presume him most secure,
> Who whether not so graced or so preferred
> As they expected, these new factions stirred.
>
> The Percys were the men, men of great might,
> Strong in alliance, and in courage strong
> That thus conspire, under pretence to right
> The crooked courses they had suffered long:
> Whether their conscience urged them or despite,
> Or that they saw the part they took was wrong,
> Or that ambition hereto did them call,
> Or others' envied grace, or rather all.
>
> What cause soever were, strong was their plot,
> Their parties great, means good, th'occasion fit:
> Their practice close, their faith suspected not,
> Their states far off and they of wary wit:
> Who with large promises draw in the Scot
> To aid their cause, he likes, and yields to it,
> Not for the love of them or for their good,
> But glad hereby of means to shed our blood.
>
> Then join they with the Welsh, who fitly trained
> And all in arms under a mighty head
> Great Glendower, who long warred, and much attained,
> Sharp conflicts made, and many vanquishèd:
> With whom was Edmund Earl of March retained
> Being first his prisoner, now confederèd,
> A man the king much feared, and well he might
> Lest he should look whether his crown stood right. . . .
>
> With these the Percys them confederate,
> And as three heads they league in one intent,
> And instituting a Triumvirate
> Do part the land in triple government:
> Dividing thus among themselves the state,
> The Percys should rule all the north from Trent,
> And Glendower, Wales; the Earl of March should be
> Lord of the south from Trent; and thus they 'gree.

The conference appears here to be among the principals, as in Shakespeare's scene (III.i), not "by their deputies" as in Holinshed's account (see note III.i, first stage direction). Daniel's account of the battle, though fairly similar to Holinshed's, heightens the valor, the characters, and the relationship of Hotspur and Hal (stanzas 99–101, 109–111):

> The swift approach and unexpected speed
> The king had made upon this new-raised force
> In th' unconfirmèd troops much fear did breed,
> Untimely hind'ring their intended course;
> The joining with the Welsh they had decreed
> Was hereby stopped, which made their part the worse,
> Northumberland with forces from the North
> Expected to be there, was not set forth.

> And yet undaunted Hotspur seeing the king
> So near approached, leaving the work in hand
> With forward speed his forces marshalling,
> Sets forth his farther coming to withstand:
> And with a cheerfull voice encouraging
> By his great spirit his well emboldened band,
> Brings a strong host of firm resolvèd might,
> And placed his troops before the king in sight.

> "This day," (say'th he) "O faithfull valiant friends,
> What ever it doth give, shall glory give:
> This day with honor frees our state, or ends
> Our misery with fame, that still shall live,
> And do but think how well this day he spends
> That spends his blood his country to relieve:
> Our holy cause, our freedom, and our right,
> Sufficient are to move good minds to fight. . . ."

> And O how well thou hadst been spared this day
> Had not wrong counselled Percy been perverse,
> Whose young undangered hand now rash makes way
> Upon the sharpèst fronts of the most fierce:
> Where now an equal fury thrusts to stay
> And rebeat back that force and his disperse,
> Then these assail, then those chase back again,
> Till stayed with new-made hills of bodies slain.

> There lo that new-appearing glorious star
> Wonder of Arms, the terror of the field
> Young Henry, labouring where the stoutest are,
> And even the stoutest forces back to yield,
> There is that hand boldened to blood and war
> That must the sword in wondrous actions wield:
> But better hadst thou learned with others' blood
> A less expense to us, to thee more good.

Hadst thou not there lent present speedy aid
To thy endangered father nearly tired,
Whom fierce-encount'ring Douglas overlaid,
That day had there his troublous life expired:
Heroical courageous Blunt arrayed
In habit like as was the king attired
And deemed for him, excused that fate with his,
For he had what his lord did hardly miss. . . .

Not only the political elements of the play but also the domestic side of the King's life, particularly his reconciliation with his son, finds some precedent in Holinshed, though the following account (III, 54–55, 1807 edn.) has obviously been subtly changed by Shakespeare in III.ii:

"The prince kneeling down before his father said: 'Most redoubted and sovereign lord and father, I am at this time come to your presence as your liege man, and as your natural son, in all things to be at your commandment. And where I understand you have in suspicion my demeanour against your grace, you know very well, that if I knew any man within this realm, of whom you should stand in fear, my duty were to punish that person, thereby to remove that grief from your heart. Then how much more ought I to suffer death, to ease your grace of that grief which you have of me, being your natural son and liege man: and to that end I have this day made myself ready by confession and receiving of the sacrament. And therefore I beseech you most redoubted lord and dear father, for the honour of God, to ease your heart of all such suspicion as you have of me, and to dispatch me here before your knees, with this same dagger. . . .'

"The king moved herewith, cast from him the dagger, and embracing the prince kissed him, and with shedding tears confessed, that indeed he had him partly in suspicion, though now (as he perceived) not with just cause, and therefore from thenceforth no misreport should cause him to have him in mistrust, and this he promised of his honour. So by his great wisdom was the wrongful suspicion which his father had conceived against him removed, and he restored to his favour. And further, where he could not but grievously complain of them that had slandered him so greatly, to the defacing not only of his honour, but also putting him in danger of his life, he humbly besought the king that they might answer their unjust accusation. . . .

"Thus were the father and the son reconciled, betwixt whom the said pickthanks had sown division, insomuch that the son upon a vehement conceit of unkindness sprung in the father, was in the way to be worn out of favour. Which was the more likely to come to pass, by their informations that privily charged him with riot and other uncivil demeanour unseemly for a prince. Indeed he was youthfully given, grown to audacity, and had chosen him companions agreeable to his age; with whom he spent the time in such recreations, exercises, and delights as he fancied. But yet (it should seem by the report of

some writers) that his behavior was not offensive or at least tending
to the damage of any body; sith he had a care to avoid doing of wrong,
and to tender his affections within the tract of vertue. . . ."

It has already been mentioned (pp. xxi–ii) that this account was
filled out by Shakespeare's knowledge of earlier plays, particularly *The
Famous Victories of Henry the Fifth.* Helpful details were suggested
by such exchanges as this from the opening scene, hinting at Gadshill's
role (II.i and ii), the Gad's Hill robbery, and the pursuit of Falstaff at
the end of II.iv:

Henry V:	How now, Jockey, what news with thee?
Jockey:	'Faith, my lord, such news as passeth, For the town of Deptford is risen With hue and cry after your man Which parted from us last night And has set upon, and hath robbed a poor carrier.
Henry V:	'Sounds, the villain that was wont to spy Out our booties.
Jockey:	Ay, my Lord, even the very same.
Henry V:	Now base-minded rascal to rob a poor carrier, Well it skills not, I'll save the base villain's life: Ay, I may: . . .

The Prince and his companion, the "Jockey," have just robbed the "receivers" (agents of Henry IV) of money they were carrying to the
Prince, here called Henry V by anticipation. The agents' embarrass-
ment at the loss of the money recalls Falstaff's account in II.iv of the
theft of the money he had previously stolen from the carriers:

Henry V:	Are you my father's receivers? Then I hope ye have brought me some money.
One [Receiver]:	Money!—alas, sir, we be robbed!
Henry V:	Robbed!—how many were there of them?
One [Receiver]:	Marry sir, there were four of them: And one of them had Sir John Old-castles bay, Hobby, And your black nag.
Henry V:	Gogs wounds!—how like you this, Jockey? 'Blood you villains: my father robbed of his money abroad, And we robbed in our stables! But tell me, how many were of them?
One [Receiver]:	If it please you, there were four of them, And there was one about the bigness of you: But I am sure I so belammed him about the shoulders, That he will feel it this month.

Henry V:	Gogs wounds!—you lammed them fairly, So that they have carried away your money.

After the withdrawal of the receivers, the Prince proposes that the
thieves adjourn to "the old tavern in Eastcheap" where there is "good
wine" and

> a pretty wench
> That can talk well, for I delight as much in their
> tongues,
> As any part about them.   [Compare I.ii.35–42.]

The fifth scene of the *Famous Victories* provides a model for the
play-acting of Falstaff and Hal in II.iv:

Enter Derick and John Cobler.

Derick:	'Sounds masters, here's ado, When princes must go to prison: Why, John, didst ever see the like?
John:	O Derick, trust me, I never saw the like.
Derick:	Why, John, thou mayst see what princes be in choler— A judge a box on the ear! I'll tell thee, John, O John, I would not have done it for twenty shillings.
John:	No, nor I, there had been no way but one with us, We should have been hanged.
Derick:	Faith John, I'll tell thee what, thou shalt be my Lord Chief Justice, and thou shalt sit in the chair, And I'll be the young prince, and hit thee a box on the ear, And then thou shalt say, to teach you what preroga- tives Mean, I commit you to the Fleet.
John:	Come on, I'll be your judge, But thou shalt not hit me hard.
Derick:	No, no.
John:	What hath he done?
Derick:	Marry, he hath robbed Derick.
John:	Why then, I cannot let him go.
Derick:	I must needs have my man.
John:	You shall not have him.
Derick:	Shall I not have my man?—say "no" and you dare! How say you?—shall I not have my man?
John:	No, marry shall you not.
Derick:	Shall I not, John?
John:	No, Derick.

Derick:	Why then take you that till more come, 'Sounds, shall I not have him?
John:	Well, I am content to take this at your hand, But I pray you, who am I?
Derick:	Who art thou, 'Sounds, dost not know thy self?
John:	No.
Derick:	Now away, simple fellow! Why man, thou art John, the cobbler.
John:	No, I am my Lord Chief Justice of England.
Derick:	Oh John! Mass, thou say'st true!—thou art indeed!
John:	Why, then to teach you what prerogatives mean, I commit you to the Fleet.
Derick:	Well I will go, but i'faith, you gray beard knave, I'll course you!

Exit. And straight enters again.
Oh John! Come, come out of thy chair!—why what a clown wert thou, to let me hit thee a box on the ear, and now thou seest they will not take me to the Fleet. . . .

Such other scenes as Falstaff's expectations of becoming Lord Chief Justice under Hal when he becomes king (I.ii.48*ff.*) are anticipated in scene vi of *The Famous Victories*, in which the Prince tells his companion Ned, "thou shalt be my Lord Chief Justice of England"—to Ned's delight: "I'll be the bravest Lord Chief Justice that ever was in England." The Prince goes on to anticipate Falstaff's view of justice in the future reign. This scene also includes the dagger episode preceding the reconciliation between the King and his son, which Holinshed describes; but in the old play, the King suggests the tears and the suspicions of Shakespeare's Henry IV (III.ii.87*ff.*, 121*ff.*) by thinking Hal has come to murder him, and weeping.

APPENDIX C
A Note on Shakespeare's English

The English of the Elizabethans, while far freer and less regular than ours, is approximately that of the present day. Modern usage, vocabulary, and spelling had by then evolved, though prevailing freedom in usage allowed much archaism and eccentricity, and only by 1700 could it be seen that the modern elements in Elizabethan English had become standard English. The standardizing process was speeded enormously by the vast influence of the printed book in England after 1500 (William Caxton introduced printing to England about 1476), and by the related growth of literacy (probably at least half the population of London could read by Shakespeare's time).

Elizabethan vocabulary was extremely adventurous. Borrowings from Latin and Greek, as well as from such fashionable modern languages as French and Italian, were encouraged by the contemporary delight in the New Learning of the Humanist translators of ancient and modern classics. Shakespeare's unusually vast vocabulary reflects this characteristic of his time. Such importations can be seen in words like Falstaff's *minions* (I.ii.23; French: *mignon*), *quiddities* (I.ii.40; Latin: *quidditas*), *iteration* (I.ii.75; Latin: *itero*), *strappado* (II.iv.203; Italian: *strappata*). These importations might or might not be anglicized in spelling, just as their pronunciation might vary. English spelling has always fluctuated between an etymological and a phonetic approach, and Elizabethan English was no exception. While most individual writers would be fairly consistent to their own style of spelling, printers would shamelessly adjust a text's spelling to suit their pages' lineation —either adding or subtracting letters, particularly final *e*'s (which were far more numerous then) and doubled consonants: *fellow* might thus also be *felow* or *felowe*. As we see in a spelling like "vniuſt," it was also customary to use *i* for *j* (and *y* was still often used where we would expect *i*), while a similar interchangeability existed between *u* and *v* until about 1630. The "long s": ſ presents no problem, as it marks no ambiguity of spelling. Though vowels now began to acquire their modern sound (particularly diphthongs), no attempt was made to distinguish similar-sounding words by spelling (as we do now with *deer* and *dear*). Similarly, some diphthongs were not yet clearly distinguished, as we see in Falstaff's pun in "If reasons were as plentiful as blackberries . . ." (II.iv.205–6), where *reason* was pronounced *raisin*. Abbreviations were far more common in manuscript than in printed books, where the most common, a stroke over a vowel, shows that a following *n* or *h* was omitted (e.g., *vpō*, printed for *upon* at I.ii.142), *yᵉ* [the] and *yᵗ* [that], where *y* = þ, the letter thorn in Old English. With such fluctuations of spelling (compare "stronds," I.i.4), pronunciation would naturally vary, but tended to follow the spelling more closely than ours. Thus, the suffix *-ion* was usually dissyllabic, and *knight* might well sound the *k*, as in the German *knabe* (though the voiced *gh* had pretty well disappeared). The alliterative effect of Hotspur's lines (IV.iii.52*ff.*) would thus be intensified by *know* and *knows*. The sound of words might well fluctuate between Chaucerian and modern pronunciation, and variations of stress in recurring uses of the same word are very apparent in Elizabethan verse. Something like the effect of the sound of Shakespeare's English might still be found in a marked British regional accent, such as that of Somerset or Yorkshire.

The grammar of Elizabethan English is highly flexible, yet approximately modern. The departures from modern norms are both numerous and slight, and the following samples culled from *Henry IV, Part 1* are representative but not comprehensive. In general, Elizabethans were more enterprising than we, using grammatical forms in experimental ways now frowned upon. Thus, adjectives were often used as adverbs: "lie too *heavy*" (IV.iii.80); and in such semi-adverbial forms as the first half of the compound "more *valiant-young*" (V.i.90). Consistency was not observed even in meaning—"more" and "most" were often used as the comparative and superlative of "great": "*More* [= greater] and less came in" (IV.iii.68). The distinction between *mo* (more numerous) and *more* (greater) also deserves note: "many mo arrivals" (IV.iv.31). Such prepositions as *in, on*, and the like were colloquially abbreviated to *a*: "What *a* Devil" (I.ii.5) = "what in the Devil['s name?]" The Anglo-Saxon intensive use of *a-* before a verb (afeared = very frightened) was extended to adjectives, as in *aweary*, (III.ii.88) = *very weary*. Many words were used adverbially in ways we no longer encounter: "would set my teeth *nothing* on edge" (III.i. 129).

Articles were often omitted—particularly before *has, is, was*, and so on: "poor jade is wrung in the withers" (II.i.6). Nouns were often used in a plural sense with a singular form: "a thousand pound" (II.iv.127) and "this seven year" (II.iv.266). In pronouns, the nominative was often favored at the expense of grammatical regularity if the rhetorical flow justified it: "I shall think the better of myself and thee during my life; *I* for a valiant champion and *thou* for a true prince" (II.iv.234–5). The genitive case presents some difficulties—the Elizabethan use of *his* as a substitute for the Middle English possessive genitive ending *-es* is well known. By contrast, certain pronouns now characteristically possessive—*your, our, their*—carried an archaic, non-possessive genitive sense. Thus "Have I not all *their* letters to meet me" (II.iii.22) means "Have I not letters of them all [saying that they will] meet me." Often the possessive genitive was marked by the use of *his* or *it* where we would now use *its* (see I.i.17–18)—and sometimes was not even marked at all: "for sport sake" (II.i.57). Other pronouns—*me, thee, him*—carry archaic dative senses (such as *by, for, with*): "And hold *me* pace in deep experiments" (III.i.47); "The sack thou hast drunk me" (III.iii.37). This extends to a reflexive dative characteristic of Falstaff's egotism: "I made me no more ado, . . . I followed me close" (II.iv.173–4, 188). A tendency also appears to add a pronoun after a name or important noun: "The skipping king he ambled up and down" (III.ii.60). The use of relative pronouns too is idiosyncratic. *Who* was used of a specific person, *which* of a kind of person, *that* after a pronoun:

> Why, Harry, do I tell thee of my foes,
> *Which* art my nearest and dearest enemy?
> Thou *that* art . . .
>
> (III.ii.122*ff.*)

Which also could be used adjectivally—"in the *which* better part" (V. iv.125)—and even to refer to a following subject:

> And, *which* became him like a prince indeed,
> He made a blushing cital of himself.
>
> (V.ii.61–2)

The archaic use of the second person singular pronoun *thou* for intimate relationships appears often in scenes between Hal and Falstaff and between Hotspur and his wife, Kate. But Kate usually talks to her husband in the more polite and serious plural form that we now all use; and Hotspur uses it to her when speaking in earnest (see II.iii. 107*ff.*).

With prepositions the Elizabethans were more casual than we are, using *in* for *on*: "*in* the neck of that" (IV.iii.92); *of* for *on*: "A plague *of* all cowards" (II.iv.100); *on* for *of*: "enamoured *on* his follies" (V.ii. 69–70), and so on. But it is the verbs that show most marked divergences from modern forms. Apart from the regular use of the second person singular, one notes the occasional preservation in the indicative of the third person singular ending in *-th* ("he confesseth," IV.iii. 47) and the occasional persistence of the old *-s* in the third person plural ending ("His letters bears his mind," IV.i.20, note). Another marked verb survival occurred in the past tenses: strong verbs now having weak forms then possessed such participles as *holp* (I.iii.13) and such preterites as *brake* (I.i.48) and *wan* (III.ii.59, note). One might note also the use of Latinate participles such as "These things you have indeed articulate" (V.i.72). Word order in questions and negatives was less standardized than now: "What say'st thou, Mistress Quickly?" (III.iii.78) would now be "What do you say [to that]?" or "What are you saying?" This last example also illustrates the weakness of Elizabethan English in the progressive or continuous forms of the present tense; the present indicative was used in many cases where we would use auxiliary forms of the present, or even the past, as in "That's the worst tidings that I *hear* of yet" (IV.i.127). The old infinitive ending *-en* was lost by Elizabethan times, allowing nouns and adjectives to be made into verbs more readily than we would now accept: "and *witch* the world" (IV.i.110). Often, the *to* also was dropped from the infinitive form: "That wished him on the barren mountains [to] starve" (I.iii.158). Elizabethans were as uncertain as moderns often are about the shades of meaning between *shall* and *will*, *should* and *would* —though their characteristic use of them may well have differed from ours. *Be* was used as a rather doubtful form of *is*: *Prince*. "I think it is good morrow, is it not?" *Sheriff*. "Indeed, my lord, I think it *be* two o'clock" (II.iv.452–3). Also, *and* (or *an*) was often used where we would expect *if*: "*And* I have not ballads made on you all, . . . let a cup of sack be my poison" (II.ii.37–8). *And if* equals *if*: "I'll break thy little finger, Harry, *And if* thou wilt not tell me" (II.iii.81–2).

Of course, many irregularities not noted here are merely the result of the demands of meter, of variation for emphasis (as in the inversion: "Richard that dead is," I.iii.145), or of characterization through idiosyncratic habits of speech—"out of all cess" (II.i.6) is the carrier's comic confusion of "out of all bounds" and "to excess." However, the most serious consideration for students of Shakespeare's language is probably the fact that Elizabethan words often had different meanings from their modern counterparts—thus, *liberty* meant "lack of restraint" (see V.ii.71, note), *presently* meant "at once," *still* meant "always," and most foreign importations kept their original senses more strongly than they now do: *apparent* (as in "heir apparent") meant "evident," not (as sometimes nowadays) "seeming"; while *aggravate* meant "make heavier," not "provoke," as now. These special meanings are carefully established in the footnotes of the present edition, as are most interesting departures from modern usage.[1]

In conclusion, worth noting are the frequent slurring and substitution of false syllables in oaths—which produce many obscure exclamations and affirmations, particularly in the prose scenes. Such softening of blasphemy is still common, though the modern allusions are less theological than the then popular "By God's wounds" or "By God's blood," usually written " 'Zounds" and " 'Sblood" in this play.

APPENDIX D
The Play's Theatrical History

Henry IV, Part 1, was probably first performed in the winter season of 1596–1597, and its immediate and continued popularity seems unmistakable. Generally accepted hearsay has it that Queen Elizabeth herself "obliged Shakespeare to write a Play of Sir John Falstaff in Love" (C. Gildon, *Remarks on the Plays of Shakespeare*, 1710), because of her delight in the character in the two histories—the result being *The*

---

[1] For a more elaborate discussion, see A. C. Baugh, *A History of the English Language* (New York, 1935). The fullest account is given in E. A. Abbott, *A Shakespearian Grammar* (London, 1869 and the many later editions). For particular words, see C. T. Onions, *A Shakespeare Glossary* (London, 1911).

Merry Wives of Windsor. After the initial performances, *Henry IV* (either one or both parts) was frequently revived. Records exist of performances of an "Oldcastle" play[1] at court for the Flemish ambassador in 1600; apparently retitled, both plays reappear at the wedding of Princess Elizabeth during the winter of 1612–1613, and Part 1 (presumably) again as *The First Part of Sir John Falstaff* at court in 1625. Reference to the performance of another "Ould Castle" play appears in court records for 1638. There were no less than nine quarto editions by 1639; and in L. Digges's preface to the 1640 edition of Shakespeare's poems it is observed that whenever the Falstaff plays are performed the audience is so crowded that "you scarce shall have roome." A clue to the nature of early performances of Hotspur's part at least (as well as to the play's popularity) is to be found in the fact that his speech on honor (I.iii.200*ff*.) is quoted in *The Knight of the Burning Pestle* (*ca.* 1609) of Francis Beaumont and John Fletcher—as an example of "a huffing part." (By contrast, John Genest, in *Some Account of the English Stage from the Restoration to 1830* [1832], praises the Hotspur of Verbruggen, at the start of the eighteenth century, as "vociferous without bellowing"!)

After the Restoration reopening of the theaters, the popularity of *Henry IV* continued, as is illustrated in the place given to Falstaff at the head of the anthology *The Wits*, published by Henry Marsh in 1662 and republished by F. Kirkman in 1672, from which the illustration on p. xviii is taken. Samuel Pepys bought a copy of the play on his way to see it performed in 1660, when it was one of the first plays revived by a restored King's Company at their opening at the Red Bull, on the return of Charles II to England. Pepys did not like it, "my expectation being too great"; but he was pleased when he saw it again in 1661, and yet again in 1667, when Falstaff's speech on honor particularly appealed to him, perhaps by contrast to the heroic plays fashionable at the time.

From about 1700 the play's continued popularity did not prevent its being cut, first by Betterton (as shown by his 1700 edition), who played Falstaff frequently, and more heavily by James Quin, who cut the extempore play-acting in II.iv. (Quin played various parts from 1718 onward). Harold Child considers that "the vogue of *Henry IV* reached its zenith in the eighteenth century" and counts two hundred and twenty performances in London from 1704 to 1750. In the first half of the nineteenth century, the play was still performed regularly by such actors as Stephen Kemble and William Macready, and it was

---

[1] However, the rivals of Shakespeare's company, the Lord Admiral's Men, did Shakespeare the compliment of imitating him in two plays about Sir John Oldcastle. These may be involved in some of the less clearly identified early performances.

treated respectfully, though Hazlitt ridiculed Kemble's performance of Falstaff in an *Examiner* review (October 1816). The play was tricked out with elaborate historical costumes and scenery by Charles Kemble in 1824, and a no less studied staging was repeated by Samuel Phelps in 1846; the battle scenes were particularly elaborate. In the later nineteenth century, the play was less popular, perhaps because the subtle interpretations of critics like Hazlitt made Falstaff too complex for performance. It was well performed by undergraduates at both Oxford and Cambridge in 1885; and another rather elaborate professional performance was staged by Beerbohm Tree, in 1896. (This performance in turn was attacked by George Bernard Shaw in the *Saturday Review*). Benson even dropped the play from his "cycle" of performances of the Histories, in both 1901 and 1906, but he performed Part 2 fourteen times at Stratford from 1894 to 1926. Another "court" performance was held in 1932 before the Prince of Wales, to celebrate the opening of the new Stratford Memorial Theater, where it has since been revived. The play has also been a regular part of the Old Vic repertory since 1917. Though less frequently performed in the United States in the early twentieth century, the play was popular here from its first performance at the Chapel Street Theater, New York, on December 18, 1761, and particularly so in the nineteenth century. It forms a natural part of the repertory of the new Shakespearean companies at Ashland, San Diego, and Stratford (Ontario).[1]

APPENDIX E
Bibliography

Shakespeare has been the subject of a great amount of writing, of greatly varying relevance and usefulness. Some sense of its range may be obtained from the relevant sections of *The Cambridge Bibliography of English Literature*, ed. F. W. Bateson (4 vols., Cambridge, England, 1941), which has a *Supplement*, ed. G. Watson (1957). More recent work in general is listed in the annual bibliographies of *The Shakespeare Quarterly* and *PMLA*. *The New Variorum Edition of Shakespeare: Henry the Fourth, Part 1*, ed. S. B. Hemingway (Philadelphia, 1936; a *Supplement* to this, by G. Blakemore Evans, is in *The Shakespeare Quarterly*, VII, 3, New York, 1956), has a good select bibliography bearing specifically on *Henry IV, Part 1*. Many of the works mentioned below have appeared in paperback editions.

[1] A more elaborate theatrical history appears in J. Dover Wilson's New Cambridge edition, but the Variorum edition has by far the most complete detailed account of performances.

For the historical background, a series of essays on social history has been collected by Sir Sidney Lee and C. T. Onions in *Shakespeare's England* (2 vols., Oxford, 1916). This is a bulky work; handier and more immediately helpful is J. Dover Wilson's anthology of extracts from writings of Shakespeare's time, *Life in Shakespeare's England* (London: Pelican, 1944). For a brief political history of the time, see S. T. Bindoff, *England Under the Tudors* (London: Pelican, 1950); but the standard work is the *Oxford History of England*.

For the history of the theater, E. K. Chambers has produced the two standard works *The Medieval Stage* (2 vols., Oxford, 1923) and *The Elizabethan Stage* (4 vols., Oxford, 1923). These books are crammed with valuable information, but are awkwardly written and exhausting to use. More accessible are G. B. Harrison's *Elizabethan Plays and Players* (Ann Arbor, 1956), and Alfred Harbage's *Shakespeare's Audience* (New York, 1961.)

Shakespeare's own life and career are again covered by a standard E. K. Chambers study, *William Shakespeare* (2 vols., Oxford, 1930). However, not much detail is known about Shakespeare's life outside his writings, and most simple chronologies cover this. For his writings, a good introduction is D. A. Traversi's *An Approach to Shakespeare* (New York, 1956), which is remarkably sane and imaginative. Also interesting is *A Companion to Shakespeare Studies*, ed. H. Granville Barker and G. B. Harrison (New York, 1960), which is a collection of essays on all aspects of Shakespeare, including a bibliography.

For the genre of history plays in general, see Irving Ribner, *The English History Play in the Age of Shakespeare* (Princeton, 1957)—a study of the genre. E. M. W. Tillyard concentrates on the Elizabethan background in *Shakespeare's History Plays* (London, 1944); L. B. Campbell stresses the context of historical theory in *Shakespeare's Histories* (San Marino, 1947); and D. A. Traversi takes a discreet New Critical approach in *Shakespeare from Richard II to Henry V* (Stanford, 1957). All three books bear directly on *Henry IV*.

The best two scholarly editions of *Henry IV, Part 1*, are J. Dover Wilson's New Cambridge (Cambridge, England, 1946), and A. R. Humphreys' new Arden edition (London, 1960), a very handy and thorough piece of work. The New Variorum edition is, like Chambers' work, very comprehensive but awkward and confusing. In addition to its material, J. Dover Wilson's article "The Origins and Development of Shakespeare's *Henry IV*," *Library*, 4th series, XXVI (Oxford, June 1945), 2–16, is helpful. For questions concerning vocabulary see C. T. Onions, *A Shakespeare Glossary* (London, 1911).

The play has drawn much critical discussion to itself, often centered on Falstaff. The part was played for farce after the Restoration, particularly by Garrick, and this provoked Maurice Morgann to write his often reprinted *An Essay on the Dramatic Character of Sir John Falstaff* in 1777 (see *Shakespeare Criticism*, ed. D. Nichol Smith, World's Classics Series, Oxford, 1916, pp. 153–189). This elaborate analysis was anticipated more discreetly by such editors as Nicholas Rowe and Samuel Johnson, but Morgann has provoked an endless debate about Falstaff's moral stature—moderns attacking his defense of Falstaff against the charge of cowardice include E. E. Stoll in his book *Shakespeare Studies* (New York, 1927) and A. C. Sprague's article "Gadshill Revisited," *Shakespeare Quarterly*, IV (April 1953), 125–137. H. B. Charlton is more sympathetic to Falstaff in his *Shakespearean Comedy* (London, 1938), and J. Dover Wilson has devoted a whole book to *The Fortunes of Falstaff* (Cambridge, England, 1946). The most brilliant modern account is possibly C. L. Barber's discussion in *Shakespeare's Festive Comedy* (Princeton, 1960), which derives Falstaff's character from medieval festival figures. B. Spivack's article "Falstaff and the Psychomachia," *Shakespeare Quarterly*, VIII (Autumn 1957), 449–459, stresses the later phases of evolution of such figures, in medieval allegory and the morality plays. A more political approach appears in two articles, H. Dickinson's about the education of a prince in "The Reformation of Prince Hal," *Shakespeare Quarterly*, XII (Winter 1938), 33–46; and Irving Ribner's "Bolingbroke, a True Machiavellian," *Modern Language Quarterly*, XI (June 1948), 177–184. A psychoanalytic approach of some interest appears in two articles in the *Psychoanalytic Quarterly*: F. Alexander's "A Note on Falstaff," II (October 1933), 592–606; and E. Kris, "Prince Hal's Conflict," XVII (October 1948), 487–506. More historically oriented are H. M. McLuhan's "Henry IV, a Mirror for Magistrates," *University of Toronto Quarterly*, XVII (January 1948), 152–160; and G. K. Hunter's "*Henry IV* and the Elizabethan Two-Part Play," *Review of English Studies*, New Series, V (August 1954), 236–248, which discusses the relationship of the two parts of the play. The play continues to excite great scholarly and critical interest.

A recording of *Henry IV (Part 1)* has been made by the Marlowe Dramatic Society, of Cambridge University: Argo, ZRG 208 to 211.

APPENDIX F
Abbreviations, References, and Editions Used in the Footnotes

AW	*All's Well That Ends Well.*
A&C	*Antony and Cleopatra.*
Beaumont and Fletcher	*Works*, ed. A. Glover and A. R. Waller, 10 vols. (Cambridge, England, 1905–1912).

Bible	References are to the Geneva (or "Breeches") Bible (1560), unless otherwise indicated.
Capell	*Mr. William Shakespeare, His Comedies, Histories, and Tragedies*, ed. E. Capell, 10 vols. (London, 1767–1768).
Cotgrave	R. Cotgrave, *A Dictionary of the French and English Tongues* (London, 1611).
Cowl	*The First Part of King Henry IV*, ed. R. P. Cowl and A. E. Morgan (Arden edn., London, 1914).
Daniel	S. Daniel, *The First Four Books of the Civil Wars Between the Two Houses of Lancaster and York* (London, 1595).
Dekker	T. Dekker, *Dramatic Works*, ed. Fredson T. Bowers, 4 vols. (Cambridge, England, 1953–1961).
Dyce	*The Works of William Shakespeare*, ed. A. Dyce, 6 vols. (London, 1857); 2nd edn., 9 vols. (1864–1867).
ed.	edited by.
edn.	edition.
F,Ff	Folio, Folios—the early collected editions of Shakespeare's plays. In this text, F (i.e., the first Folio's) readings are usually followed by all later Folio editions' readings.
Famous Victories	Anon., *The Famous Victories of Henry the Fifth, Containing the Honorable Battle of Agincourt* (London, 1958). (See Hemingway, for a modern reprinting.)
1HIV	*Henry IV, Part 1.*
2HIV	*Henry IV, Part 2.*
HV	*Henry V.*
Ham	*Hamlet.*
Harvey	Gabriel Harvey, *Complete Works*, ed. A. B. Grosart, 3 vols. (London, 1884–1885).
Hemingway	*Henry the Fourth Part I*, ed. S. B. Hemingway (New Variorum edn., Philadelphia, 1936).
Holinshed	R. Holinshed, *Chronicles of England, Scotland and Ireland*, 6 vols. (London, 1807–1808). (Shakespeare probably used the 2nd edn., 1587).
Humphreys	*The First Part of King Henry IV*, ed. A. R. Humphreys (new Arden edn., London, 1960).
JC	*Julius Caesar*
Kittredge	*The First Part of King Henry the Fourth*, ed. G. L. Kittredge (Boston, 1940).

Lear	*King Lear.*
LLL	*Love's Labour's Lost.*
Lyly	John Lyly, *Complete Works*, ed., R. W. Bond, 3 vols. (Oxford, 1902).
Malone	*The Plays and Poems of William Shakespeare*, ed. E. Malone, 10 vols. (London, 1790).
Measure	*Measure for Measure*
MND	*A Midsummer Night's Dream.*
Nashe	Thomas Nashe, *Works*, ed. R. B. McKerrow, 5 vols. (London, 1904–1910).
NCS	*The First Part of the History of Henry IV*, ed. John Dover Wilson (New Cambridge Shakespeare edn., Cambridge, England, 1946).
OED	*A New English Dictionary*, ed. J. A. H. Murray *et al.*, 13 vols. (Oxford, 1884–1928).
Oth	*Othello.*
Pope	*The Works of Shakespeare*, ed. Alexander Pope, 6 vols. (London, 1725; 2nd edn., 10 vols., 1728).
Q,Qq	Quarto, Quartos—small, early single play editions.
RII	*Richard II.*
RIII	*Richard III.*
Rowe	*The Works of Mr. William Shakespeare*, ed. N. Rowe, 7 vols. (London, 1709; 3rd edn., 8 vols., 1714).
S.D.	Stage direction(s).
Shakespeare	All references to other Shakespearean plays are keyed to *The Tudor Shakespeare*, ed. Peter Alexander (London, 1951).
Shrew	*The Taming of the Shrew.*
Steevens	*The Plays of William Shakespeare*, ed. I. Reed (with notes by G. Steevens), 15 vols (London, 1793).
Stow	J. Stow, *A Survey of London* (London, 1598; enlarged 1603, 1613).
Temp	*The Tempest.*
Theobald	*The Works of Shakespeare*, ed. L. Theobald, 7 vols. (London, 1733; 2nd edn., 8 vols., 1740).
Titus	*Titus Andronicus.*
TN	*Twelfth Night.*
T&C	*Troilus and Cressida.*
Warburton	*The Works of Shakespeare*, ed. W. Warburton, 8 vols. (London, 1747).